WHAT ARE THEY SAYING ABOUT
THEOLOGICAL METHOD?

What Are They Saying About Theological Method?

J. J. Mueller, S.J.

PAULIST PRESS
New York/Ramsey

Library of Congress
Catalog Card Number: 84-61031

ISBN: 0-8091-2657-5

Published by Paulist Press
545 Island Road, Ramsey, N.J. 07446

Printed and bound in the
United States of America

Contents

Preface

A method is a tool. Like a good multi-purpose screwdriver, a method improves upon what weak fingers and fragile fingernails cannot do. A method extends our abilities, improves upon our limitations, reminds us of forgotten procedures, and allows others to see how we arrived at our conclusions.

Method is not something that we reflect on as such; usually we concern ourselves with finding solutions to immediate problems. But whenever we ask ourselves how we arrived at the answer, then we are raising the method question. Method is done best by reflecting over how we actually arrived at an answer. Method then reflects upon reflecting.

Theologians who discuss method are a small number. They can be compared to computer scientists who develop new designs for computers. Very few of us know the names of scientists who conceived the idea to build computers, improve them, and make new advances. Perhaps a few more of us know the names of companies who produce them (e.g., IBM, Xerox, Apple) and what features each offers. But every one of us experiences the effects of computers whether we play video games, buy food at a grocery store, drive an automobile, or work in an office.

In theology, very few of us might know the name of Karl Rahner or John Macquarrie, a few more of us might know what a transcendentalist or existentialist method is, but every one of us has benefited from their insights whether in sermons, pastoral care units in hospitals, liturgy, or *Time* magazine articles discussing current topics in Christianity.

My task is to tell you what theologians are saying about theological method. Because method never sits apart from the theologian who wields it or from the content of theology that is generated, the task is a challenging one. Every area of theological method cannot be covered: scriptural exegesis deserves a book of its own, ethics another. I will limit method to those theologians who try to explain theology as a whole and the relationships of its parts. Theologians refer to this area as systematic theology and are called systematic theologians.

In the past, systematic theology was uniform in method. Scripture, for instance, was used to support the teachings (doctrines and dogmas). Scripture appeared as a proof text and not something to be studied for itself. At the end of the nineteenth century, the philosophy of Thomas Aquinas and the Scholastics who followed him was virtually the only acceptable basis for theology. In the first half of the twentieth century, historical investigations unearthed a variety of differences within Thomism itself and opened up the possibility of diversity as part of the Catholic Christian tradition. By the time of Vatican II, the recognition of a plurality of methods arrived. The 1970's was a decade of books on method which indicated a new transition in how theology was done. Indeed, a real change was taking place that will have far-reaching consequences for theology both in this century and in the one to come. In brief, a pluralism with regard to method has been achieved. Truth exceeds one method's grasp. While uniformity of method has been superseded by a plurality, the question of unity remains. Thus every theologian must be clear about his or her starting point, presuppositions, and consequences for theology. This is what method tries to do.

Within systematic theology, I have chosen four representative methods: transcendental, existential, empirical, and socio-phenomenological. Since a method cannot be separated from the theologian who uses it, I will present such a representative theologian. At the same time, because people use method differently, I will present two theologians who use the same method but in two different ways to show the diversity of method. Each theologian will be asked three questions: (1) Because each theologian uses method differently, what is the vision of theology each is concerned with (and this will include the starting point for doing theology)? (2) Because method and content go together, what is the step by step presentation of how the method works? (3) Because we should benefit from their findings, what difference does its consequences make for our lives today? By coordinating method, theologian, and theology, the reader can become intelligently aware of what theologians are saying about theological method.

Finally, I would like to dedicate this book to the John Courtney Murray Jesuit writers' group and the Jesuit community of Gonzaga University who have so patiently encouraged me.

J. J. Mueller, S.J.
St. Louis University
St. Louis, Missouri
January 1984

1
How Do I Encounter God Today?
Transcendental Method:
Rahner and Lonergan

What is the main concern of theology? Sin? Salvation? Belief in God? Belief in Jesus Christ? We would want to include all of these within a theology. But is there some fundamental relationship that holds these together, prioritizes them in order of importance, and makes a claim as the primary concern for theology? Yes. Theology begins in the God-human relationship. If this fundamental relationship does not exist, then we are left alone as exiles on this earth to grope through life. Any theology would be meaningless.

Our first method for investigation is used by two theologians, Karl Rahner and Bernard Lonergan, who concern themselves with this fundamental relationship. In the form of a question, they express this relationship as: can the human person encounter God today? Through what is called a transcendental method, they focus upon the human person as radically (i.e., "from the roots") open to God. Transcendental refers to the capacity to go beyond ourselves ("trans"). Rahner writes more generally of how we go beyond ourselves through knowledge and freedom, Lonergan more specifically of how we do it

5

through understanding and conversion. Since the time of the philosopher Kant, "transcendental" has also carried the technical meaning of grasping "the conditions for the possibility of . . ."[1] Both Rahner and Lonergan include Kant's philosophical meaning. While both theologians use a transcendental method, they differ in their application of it. Just as a screwdriver can be used as a tool to pry open a can or turn a screw, so too can the same theological method, in the hands of two different people, be used in two different ways. Through their use of transcendental method, Rahner and Lonergan have developed two of the most influential theologies today.

Karl Rahner

The German Jesuit Karl Rahner (1904–1984) is arguably the most important theologian of the last half of the twentieth century. His insights have dominated Catholic theology in particular. He has offered fresh insights into the God-human relationship through his expression of the human openness to God. By referring to his theology as "theological anthropology," he underscores the human person as the arena where the encounter with God takes place. Since we cannot escape being human, we cannot unfold the mystery of God's encounter with us except from the vantage point of our humanity. We remain inside participants discovering God's ways with us. If our humanity is the medium through which God communicates with us, then what is said about us says something about God who is involved with us. As human beings we become the condition for the possibility of an encounter with God. By making explicit what is implicit in our humanity, or thematizing the unthematized, we can understand God's words to us. Hence, by penetrating our humanity (anthropology), we open ourselves to understanding God's involvement with us (theology).

Our task will be to put the following questions to Rahner. How does he develop his vision of theology? How does his transcendental method proceed step by step? And what does his method say to us today?

Rahner's *Foundations of Christian Faith*[2] (1976) represents in one volume more than a quarter century of outstanding publications. Asking him to reflect on the God-human relationship, he would say that the starting point for theology can be nothing less than human experience taken as a whole. We are people thrown into the current of history, with a long ancestry of people and events that have shaped our present day and whose dynamics we feel. We experience ourselves as people in time and place. We can only ask questions from within this limited horizon. Likewise our perspective of knowledge is limited by this horizon. Yet for all our limitations, human persons seem to go beyond time and place to grasp the meaning of life itself. For example, the human being, in every age, asks questions. The structure of knowledge goes beyond this time and place and implies that there are answers. In such a basic activity as asking questions the human being, through knowledge, goes beyond himself or herself to the meaning of life itself as grasped within my particular history. Just as a keyhole can tell us something about the kind of key that fits it, so too our radical openness tells us something about what our humanness is and why we are the way we are. Hence the answer of human living is not satisfied on the biological level but it reaches out so that our spirits seek spiritual fulfillment. We are open to the mystery which grounds all meaning. This mystery is God.[3]

The greatest question remains ourselves.[4] We are a mystery to ourselves. We also bear ultimate responsibility for the answer. Whereas I can escape other questions, the question of myself I cannot elude. Through responsible and free choices, which in a sense we are forced to make, we build our lives and provide the answer to who we are. As long as we live we never reach a final answer, because as we continually grow, we are always determining ourselves. Death alone is the ending to this earthly life and so we can rightly say that we live toward death.

Our freedom and knowledge tells us that we are open to fulfillment of spirit. As Augustine said so well, "Our hearts are made for you, O Lord, and we are restless until they rest in you." Sometimes this "more" of reality that Rahner calls mystery is experienced as a feeling of being grasped. It may come from a sunset, the birth of a baby, a death, or being in love. Above all the experience is an irreducible mystery wherein God has communicated to us who we are. This is a religious experience and simultaneously the answer to ourselves as questions.

Since this mystery (God) spoke to us about who he is, we are dealing with what we call revelation. Only God himself can tell us truthfully who he is. By initiating the conversation, God would have to speak freely; we could not force him. Through revelation we find that he wants to speak to us, that he converses for our sake, and that he cares if we listen or not. But he will not force us to respond to him against our freedom. Nevertheless our freedom finds its true meaning only by freely responding to him. Our well-being (salvation) and happiness will result.

In the Christian experience of revelation in Jesus Christ, God not only told us that he was inextricably bound with us through love but he also showed us what it means to live in this love by the word becoming flesh.[5] As divine, or, as St. Paul says, as "the image of the invisible God" (Col 1:15), he is the revealer of God's love par excellence; as human, he is the hearer of God's word par excellence. Thus if we want to know what God is like and how he has involved himself with us, then we look to Jesus. Likewise if we want to know what humanity is like and how we are involved with God, then we look to Jesus. Using spatial imagery, whether our perspective is from the divine above or from the human below, Jesus Christ is the unique meeting place of the God-human relationship. The implications of this fundamental reality branch out to every nook and cranny of theology.

On the one hand, the revelation of Jesus is constrained by a particular history. It remains situated in time at about 30 A.D. and in a place between Galilee and Jerusalem in the Middle East. On the other hand, the revelation of Jesus escapes any particular history and continues as true for us today as it was then. Only our relationship, not the content, has changed. Instead of encountering a Jesus who walks and talks with us, who not so incidentally was rejected by many who saw and heard him, we encounter his words and deeds recorded in Scripture and the experiences of Christian believers who have verified his revelation over two thousand years. As in the first century, so now in the twentieth, we authenticate in our own lives the revelation of Jesus. The Father of Jesus who loved us into life and calls us to himself continues to speak his word to us. History then finds its fullest meaning in Christ and theology reflects upon the implications.

Jesus is not someone who adds another dimension (supernatural) to being human like stacking one block on top of another. On the contrary, humanity finds itself perfected in its humanness precisely in Jesus. The completion of the human quest for happiness is God himself. Instead of the image of blocks being added to one another, an organic image of evolutionary growth toward God better expresses the reality—e.g., like a seed that becomes a tree through growth and change even though the seed is not the full grown tree. So too is the biological, psychological, and spiritual person called into fuller transformation in Christ by God. Whether expressed negatively—anthropology is deficient Christology—or positively—Christology completes anthropology—the reality is the same. Humanity finds its meaning in Christ.

Theologically Rahner characterizes a human being as a "hearer of the word."[6] "Hearing" goes beyond sound to the per-

sonal encounter of a presence. What we hear are not words but
God's own self communicated. The analogy is not so much two
people who talk together, but two people who fall in love—one
self hears or encounters another self in free self-donation.
Speaking and hearing represent a scriptural metaphor which
expresses God's involvement with us. The not so metaphorical
theological word for this self-communication is the word
"grace." As self-donation grace is always freely given and calls
forth our free acceptance. The result is mutual self-donation
which is love. Grace should not be conceived of as a quantity of
something like a plastic packet of powder delivered by parcel
post to my door but rather along the lines of an interpersonal
model where a person, like a human lover, becomes involved
with me: my hopes, aspirations, sufferings, dreams, loves—my
life. As two people who love another do not lose their respective
identities but really enhance them, so God communicates himself and remains the totally other shrouded in unfathomable
mystery that is never exhausted. Our relationship always invites
continued love and involvement ahead.

Let us now bring together the various elements of the
vision of theological anthropology into a step by step examination of how the transcendental method works. (1) A problem,
task, or concern arises when we have a question. Every question
implies that we as human beings are already involved. The
question itself stems from life experiences. Thus Rahner begins
from the anthropological side and describes the human question. Taking experience as a whole, he uses the findings of science, philosophy, literature, and theology to describe the question. Whatever concerns human beings becomes subject matter
for theology. (2) By asking what are the conditions for the possibility of understanding this question for us as human beings
(i.e., transcendentally), particularly through knowledge and
freedom, he presents our radical openness to God. Through
what we know and the exercise of our freedom to make the

truth part of our dynamically developing history, we become more authentically human, and the meaning of who we are orients us to God. So far, the process is one of making the implicit explicit, the unthematized thematized. At this point, the revelation of Jesus becomes a factor and allows us to know of God's involvement with us in the relationship. (3) As the primary Christian revelation which requires acceptance on faith, Jesus Christ reveals God and how we are to respond. Both in history and through his Spirit, Jesus continues to reveal the Father and our response. The revelation is mediated through the believing community, Scripture, dogma, doctrine, devotions, prayer, and religious experiences. (4) Finally, Rahner pulls together the anthropological question and the theological interpretation to explain how the results can be understood today and thereby help us live our lives of faith. In a mutually informing relationship of human experience and divine revelation understood theologically, the question has an answer for today.

While these steps are the bare bones of his method, it can become quite complicated and sophisticated in its use, as readers of Rahner will testify. What is unaccounted for in his method is the breadth and depth of his own scholarship which seems a perfect match for his powerful method. All the while Rahner is straightforward and clear both in his presuppositions and his use of them. Thus others can share in his search and test his conclusions.

As we take our leave from Rahner, we ask ourselves our last question: What has Rahner's theological method said to us?

First of all, Rahner's transcendental method has located the starting point for theology in the human person. Previous to Rahner, sometimes theology had given the impression of having the answers and needing only our particular questions. With Rahner, the human person is inextricably bound up with the question and whatever helps to explain human experience as a whole is grist for the theological mill. Thus science is not a threat per se to faith but a partner.

Theology looks less like a set of beliefs chiseled on stone tablets to which people look to as unchanging and more like a dynamic relationship interacting with God's Spirit on the cutting edge of history. As historical people we are the arenas where the encounter takes place and the ones who must respond. In this sense all theology is anthropology.

Second, Rahner's theology is extremely Christocentric. Anthropology finds its most complete expression of meaning in Jesus Christ, and God's word reveals itself most clearly in Jesus. As true God and true man Jesus illuminates the definitive nature of the God-human relationship. Because Rahner relies upon the revelation of the word made flesh, his Christology can be referred to as incarnational. Spiritually, then, to be Christian is to incarnate God within our flesh. The human becomes divine. Our life is a constant task of becoming transformed into God's holy and loving mystery. By imitating in our lives what Christ was in his incarnation, we also expect to share in his passion and death. The cost of discipleship is total fidelity to God. Likewise, all that is true of the glorified humanity of Christ will be true for us in proportion to our response.

Rahner's Christology is the center of his theology and organizes his theological investigations. Like planetary orbits which overlap each other, dogma, doctrine, devotions, prayers, liturgy, Mariology, and everything else in theology is systematized according to the revelation of Jesus as the center of faith's gravity. Hence, if they are properly done, devotions to the saints should put us more in contact with Jesus Christ who leads us to the Father and enhance our love of neighbor.

Third and finally, Rahner's theology is evolutionary and hopeful. Jesus has sealed the victory of the human race forever over sin. God's grace and our free response now work together to allow us to become the persons God calls us to be. The process is "hominisation" (humanization)—i.e., becoming more and more Christlike through becoming more and more human. Through our cooperation, all creation responds in giving birth to a Spirit-filled world. Everything has meaning and by our cooperation organically evolves through history to greater inclusion in God himself. With Irenaeus, Rahner agrees that "the glory of God is man fully alive" but would add "and man fully alive is man knowing and loving God." If we authentically become responsible for our humanity, we will find that God has been walking at our side all the time and calling us to himself. To our humble amazement God is closer than we imagined.

Bernard Lonergan

Because Karl Rahner's theological anthropology has dominated Catholic theology his work sets the pace for theologians to follow. While the theologians in this book and elsewhere know of Rahner's work, even depend and dialogue with him in some cases, they are not necessarily dependent upon him. Even if Rahner's name is not a household word, his use by other theologians as a dialogue partner is one of the greatest testimonies of his significance. He situates other theologians by his contribution and sounds the tone of contemporary theology since Vatican II by which other theologies and methods are judged. Like an all-star defensive middle linebacker in football, no offense can ignore his constant presence and ability to ferociously tackle weak theological runners.

Both Rahner's inadequacies and contributions come to the foreground when other theologians develop their own methods. The Canadian Jesuit Bernard Lonergan (1904–   ) was molded by the same influences as Rahner in transcendental method but developed in a slightly different direction and with another application. His book *Method in Theology*[7] (1972) offers a remarkable enterprise or agenda for doing theology in the contemporary scientific world and it remains to be fully implemented.

Lonergan understands theology to mediate between a cultural matrix and the significance and role of a religion in that matrix. The mind is the liaison which opens up the relationship. Transcendental method is a normative pattern of recurrent and related operations of the mind which yield cumulative and progressive results. It is transcendental method because the results are not confined to a particular field or subject. Where other methods aim at meeting the needs proper to a particular field, transcendental method is concerned with meeting the needs and exploiting the opportunities presented by the human mind itself.[8] We all know and observe transcendental method to the extent that we are attentive, intelligent, reasonable, and responsible. Thus the transcendental method heightens one's consciousness by objectifying it. We become more authentic persons in possession of ourselves through understanding.

If we asked Lonergan's help to understand theological method, he might begin by reminding us that we have already asked the basic question: we want to search for meaning by understanding. Theology always implies an act of understanding. Indeed, if the definition of theology is faith seeking understanding, then we must pay attention to how we know, what we know when we know, and how we know that we know. Human knowing is the place to begin.

The operations of the mind do not proceed in any random form. The dynamic process of knowing always operates the same way: experiencing, understanding, judging, and deciding.[9] Experience gives rise to understanding which leads to a judgment about the truth of what is presented and finally is acted upon. For example, I may be angry with my brother. My experience of anger is handed over to understanding which asks why. I understand that it is not my brother who is the cause of my anger but, rather, before meeting my brother, I had an argument with someone. My frustration boiled over into anger which I vented upon the next person who happened to be my brother. My judgment acknowledges that the previous fight and not my brother is the cause, so I decide to apologize to my brother for my angry and misplaced outburst. If I had stayed in the anger and not raised questions, known the truth of what I acted upon and not changed my activity toward my brother, a harmful event for everyone concerned would have continued. Moreover each function of the mind needed the other to finish what the previous function could not do. Experience cannot judge, understanding cannot decide, etc. Lonergan is a firm debunker of the popular saying that what you see is what you get. For data resists taking a good look. Truth does not come from appearances any more than understanding.

A pilot once told me that the hardest but most necessary skill he had to learn was to trust his flight instruments. Relying upon one's sense of gravity or appearances or feelings in a spinning plane will be disastrous. A Concorde jet or lunar spaceship about to land is too sophisticated and complex to be entrusted to human perceptions. We constantly rely on instruments and measuring apparatus to help us understand. Even in our technological age, by human perception the earth still looks flat, a stick plunged in water appears bent, and people's actions are misjudged as insincere. Only by sifting the data, understanding, judging, and deciding can we take authentic responsibility for our lives.

Data has many shapes, sizes, and colors. For instance, atoms are not solid particles but mostly space; heavy objects do not fall faster in a vacuum. Data which is the raw stuff of experience is not univocal so that everyone can merely look at it and arrive at the same conclusions. So too does that apply to the entire act of understanding. Why does one person see Jesus as Savior and another regard him as a blasphemer? How can Jesus be adored by some and a folly to others? How can we have disciples and heretics, believers and non-believers coming from the same experience? The act of understanding is the key.

No matter at what level, if a blockage occurs, it must be changed. Lonergan calls this "conversion." It is the center of his theological method. This important concept brings his theory of knowing into the theological sphere. Conversion takes place on four levels related to the four levels of the act of understanding: affective (experience),[10] intellectual (understanding), moral (judging), and religious (deciding). Like the act of understanding, these four conversions are interconnected and dynamically related. To be an integrated person requires a fourfold conversion. For example, someone who loves (affective), and does what is right (moral) and loves God (religious) but who thinks that everyone is going to hell is in need of an intellectual conversion. Faulty information about the revelation of God in Jesus Christ is a blockage that affects one's life. Moreover any conversion is interrelated such that a change in any one of the levels will require the other levels to reassess themselves.

Even if one already believes, one must continually be open to the fourfold conversion. Christian life is ongoing conversion, dynamically lived and developing. For example, as one attends college where new intellectual subjects are presented, changes on the affective, moral, and religious levels are to be expected. Or, on another level, as one enters into a love relationship such as marriage, one can expect changes to occur on the intellectual, moral, and religious levels. Ongoing conversion, and not just a one-time conversion, is the manner by which we live authentic lives.

How then does Lonergan's method proceed step by step? As the world becomes more diverse, and pluralisms in thought more acceptable, Lonergan offers the art of understanding as a unity which cuts across any discipline. Based upon his philosophy, Lonergan develops a method for doing theology according to the functional specialties (experience, understanding, judgment, decision). Functional specialties now designate the various tasks of the theologian. What might at first seem like a complicated system is relatively easy to comprehend.[11] There are eight functional specialties: research, interpretation, history, dialectic, foundations, doctrine, systematics, and communications. Each corresponds to one operation of human knowing.

(Decision:)	Dialectic→Foundation	
(Judgment:)	History	Doctrine
(Understanding:)	Interpretation	Systematics
(Experience:)	Research	Communications

Hence, research corresponds to experience (gather the data), interpretation corresponds to understanding (understands what is meant), history corresponds to judgment (makes specific and precise the human activities in their geographical distribution and temporal succession), and dialectic corresponds to decision (seeks a comprehensive viewpoint to examine conflicts). These four functional specialties hand over their data to the following four functional specialties which deal precisely with the faith content of theology. Foundations, like dialectics, corresponds to the function of decision and deals with Christian conversion which is the horizon within which the meaning of doctrines can be apprehended. Doctrine, like history, corresponds to judgment of facts and values. Fact and values affirmed give rise to further questions of the truth of doctrinal expressions or their inconsistency or fallacy. Systematics, like interpretation, attempts to work out appropriate systems of conceptualization, to remove apparent inconsistencies, and to move toward the comprehensive grasp of theology. Communications, like research, corresponds to experience and is concerned with theology in its external relations.

Each step is dynamically interrelated to what goes before and after. To skip one of the steps results in a curtailment of the fullness of human meaning and offers insufficient and erroneous conclusions. For example, fundamentalists who allow no questions to be asked and rely exclusively upon faith in the words of the Scripture truncate the responsibility of a human being to think. For them, Scripture is as clear as reading the morning newspaper. Asking questions and judging the truth or falsity of an interpretation reaching over several cultures and encompassing twenty centuries is not allowed. Theology, if it is to serve people today, should not dehumanize one by taking away reason. Lonergan affirms that God has gifted me with the ability of reason for the purpose of drawing closer to God by living authentically.

Lonergan has thematized what already existed as functions of the human mind. Since each function has a specific purpose, theology can do well to follow these natural functions of the mind in devising its own method and build upon them. Anyone can enter into the process but only those in faith will live it. Even if one prefers another schema, according to Lonergan human knowing must be dealt with. This is his challenge to theology.

The act of knowing is not an isolated motor geared toward knowledge alone. Knowledge is part of the larger human whole of being in love. The end of the human person is not to know but to love. A Christian, for Lonergan, is one who is in love. Conversion to love on the four levels is a call to total giving of the self in an integrated way. Even in the face of suffering and pain, the authenticity of the human person comes in the meaning of love. The human person is oriented toward Jesus Christ in a relationship of faith-filled love and hope.

Like Rahner, Lonergan places great responsibility on the human person before God and others. Penetrating to the truth of our lives is not a simple task. It takes responsibility aided by faith. Coming to understand ourselves and the world around us is a way of coming to know God and how he deals with us. When all is said and done, understanding allows us to be free to love God and others more deeply. This love is affective, intellectual, moral, and religious. It remains open to continual conversion as the relationship dynamically develops. Lonergan moves from the human mind to a method for theology. He suggests a correspondence of functional specialties that complete human knowing communally as well as individually. How can he justify the use of the part for the whole, one individual mind as application for a community of minds?

What is Lonergan's contribution to theology? Lonergan's work is in the process of still being evaluated. It is like a giant enterprise to be undertaken. Hence his contribution, although already significant, remains to be finally judged.

Lonergan, like Rahner, is a theologian who centers his theology on the human person's dynamic openness and orientation to God in Christ. Whereas Rahner prefers religious experience to be tested and illumined by the revelation of Christ, Lonergan prefers to start with the dynamic act of knowing as the starting point. If Rahner's vision of the believer is a hearer of God's word, then Lonergan's is the one who undergoes constant conversion to love. For both theologians, love of God in Christ as found in humanity remains the fundamental teaching of Christ and gives identity to human persons.

Lonergan has worked out a more detailed method than Rahner that suggests a team approach to doing theology. No one person can be an expert in the eight functional specialties. As time and theology develop, we acquire more and more knowledge within a highly specialized field and less and less about how to combine the fields together. Aware of this pluralism, Lonergan offers a challenging enterprise of interrelating the various parts of the whole which will take time to implement. In a sense, he is a theologian of the future.

Rahner's method is strongly Christocentric and relies upon the interpretation of ourselves and God's revelation in Christ. Perhaps less artistic and more similar to the way science discovers and tests data, Lonergan's method is conversion centered. Together, Rahner and Lonergan present a transcendental method that looks at the human person's openness to God. Beginning from two different starting points—for Rahner it is theological anthropology, for Lonergan it is the act of understanding—they both use the same method but with slightly different emphases and applications so that even within a common consensus about method, different theologies result. Without doubt, and within Catholic theological circles in particular, Rahner and Lonergan are two of the most formidable theological figures.

2
Does the World Around Me Matter? Existential Method: Macquarrie and Tillich

Knowledge and freedom as dealt with by Rahner and Lonergan open the person to the possibility of God's life. This optimistic use of knowledge and freedom is only one side of the coin because knowledge and freedom can be, on the other side, a source of anguish and pain. The statement that every virtue has its vice expresses the dual drive of any possibility. Freedom and knowledge require use and theology imposes responsibility upon the person. A certain urgency can exist in the responsibility. For example, the difference between "I see a tree" and "That tree is about to fall on me" leaves no doubt on the feeling level of a panic running through me. I am not a disinterested observer in the world but a living participant who is affected. Because I care, the world around me matters.

The next method that we will address is existentialism. In that their methods begin from questions springing up from human existence, the next two theologians are existentialists. However, one cannot stop with that as a final description of their respective methods. The first, John Macquarrie from England, seeks to define how theology proceeds from existential to ontological categories within a believing and responsible tradition of faith. The second, Paul Tillich, a German-born theologian who spent most of his years teaching in the United States, seeks to bring together apparently contradictory and complicated relationships in his method of correlation. Both methods speak to modern people's feelings arising from anxiety, alienation, fear, boredom, and confusion. Their contribution has been the immersion of theology into the secular world of experience in order to draw out theology's relevance and thereby address itself to the modern world. Theology, far from losing its relevancy, becomes a suitable dialogue partner for the modern world and an indispensable source of truth to all people. Through primarily clear modern interpretations of the faith for today, both these theologians generate an entire systematic theology.

John Macquarrie

The term existential is important to both theologians because they describe their own methods by it. Macquarrie refers to his method as existential-ontological while Tillich calls his a method of correlation that uses existential questions and Christian answers. Existential means existence or reality as we personally experience it right now. Feelings play an important part because they evaluate the concerns about which we seek answers in order to live authentically human lives. Alienation, determinism, powerlessness, dread, fear, anxiety, and coming death are common experiences used by these authors. The emphasis, as it must, falls upon the existing individual living in the world. Intersubjectivity, the importance of the body, freedom and choice are constant themes running throughout their work. Thus the present moment is the starting point of their analysis.

   The Anglican theologian John Macquarrie in his systematic theology (*Principles of Christian Theology,*[1] 1977) brings
together the contemporary experience, Christian teaching from
the past, and relates it to the present believing community,
through an existential-ontological method. This method does
what it says: beginning with an analysis of the changing existential situation for which all manners and means of contemporary scientific knowledge can be used, Macquarrie looks to
what is beyond the change to what endures. The developing situation is subjected to continuity of truth as found in Christian
faith to yield the ontological factor. Ontological indicates what
stands behind the particulars of existence.[2] For example, the
existential problem of believing in God stems from many
sources, one of which is that science has discovered and con-
trolled nature. Controlling nature was formerly attributed only
to God. Thus this God who was needed as controller of nature
is effectively dead. The human being is the power manipulator
now.

   Macquarrie would begin with this description of controlling nature as the existential fact but look to whether or not
Christian revelation would have anything further to say about
it. What Macquarrie discovers to have emerged is a false notion
of God. God is not defined as the sustainer of physical laws.
That concept of "God" is rightfully dead and, like a patient par-
ent who waits for the child to grow up, God has awaited the
human race's developing emergence to fuller humanization
whereby we accept co-responsibility for the universe. At the
same time we find that God is emancipated from our projections
to disclose who he really is. Far from dead, God is vibrantly
alive and invites us to further participate in his creation. The
ontological reality is not an image of God as the stage manager
who does everything himself but as the drama itself (beginning,
middle, and end) who calls us to act in concert with him. In a
true sense, the disclosure of the real God comes about by our

developing capacity to experience him for who he is. Hence, specific existents are not to be confused with the source of existence itself. Hence Macquarrie makes the distinction between existents which are beings and existence which is Being itself— or the difference between props put on stage for the drama and the drama itself. God is Being and is manifested through beings. Our story becomes God's story and God's story is our story. Macquarrie operates his method by moving from beings (existential analysis) to Being itself (ontological analysis).

Macquarrie's method does not stop with an explanation of one experience. Every experience, if it is oriented toward God, should connect with others. Hence the organization of answers should not contradict one another but be related and even increase our knowledge when held together. Balanced teachings require finding the many relationships between teachings and life. This is the area of systematic theology. Since all theology looks to the manifestation of God, then it is a symbolic theology. Nothing in nature, not even the human person, is God but always a manifestation or symbolization of God who undergirds life itself. God is the one who lets be. We beings form and express Being by sharing in God's life responsibly. Macquarrie relies upon the symbolic nature of reality as a presupposition of faith.

One additional and important element of method that he specifically emphasizes is the role of the traditional teaching community as interpreter of the existential-ontological reality. The community has teachings or doctrines which have gathered up these great interpretations of history and serves the community today with them. The believing community possesses a wealth of interpretation that has been handed down through the centuries by lived experience. While in history the Church's teachings are always couched in space and time, language and expression, nevertheless the expressions themselves bear witness to the ontological reality of their existential situations. Since this is so, these teachings transcend their encapsulations and serve as helps to deepen, penetrate, and enrich the understanding of God's salvific presence today.

Since no contemporary expression can say everything for the believing community, the community acts to steady the course through a roughened sea. Then the communal experience united by God will allow theology to speak and have power. Macquarrie understands his Anglican legacy as a via media that strikes a balance between Catholic and Protestant emphases in theology. Balancing a Catholic theologian like Rahner on the one side and the existential demythologization of a Bultmann on the other, Macquarrie finds the middle ground. Indeed, balance seems to be the most characteristic feature of his theological vision.

Macquarrie's existential-ontological method seeks to remove the barrier between human experience and God's presence. God is not a god of church buildings but one immersed in the present worldly experience of every man and woman. The problem is finding God in this world. Macquarrie suggests that finding God implies looking for him in the everyday situations. If one looks beyond the ordinary, perhaps one will see the extraordinary. Like windows which let us look outside the confines of our solid walls, the transparency of beings can disclose Being. Far from being wishful Romanticism, this view acknowledges that the existential moments of pain as well as the joy, suffering as well as the triumphs, anxiety as well as security are two-edged and can reveal God's activity. Humanness is not to be too tightly defined in terms of joy, happiness and health; suffering, sorrow, and sickness are not of themselves barriers from God's loving disclosures of himself. Based on the faith commitment of us to God and God to us, Macquarrie's method looks to the holiness of the present moment to see God's continual invitation at work.

On the one hand, Macquarrie's method interprets experience and refrains from judging a person for having experiences that are negative, humanly dependent, unnerving, even bordering on the absurd. These are human experiences and therefore proper topics for theology. His method of entering into the existential here-and-now pain to bring out the riches of belief is his strength. Theology, on the other hand, not only interprets experience but also responds to human experience. Fed by new experiences theology becomes richer and operates at its best—a help to the human heart to make total faith commitment. Only in the face of conflict is belief challenged. To use a modern cliché, if theology cannot take the heat then it must get out of the kitchen. If it cannot address the pain and frustration of modern people then it has nothing to say to the world. Its relevancy is gone. Far from undercutting theology or its methods, modern people's predicament enlivens the importance of the good news of Jesus. What seemed like old news to some turns out to be good news as fresh as the first Christians' experience. Theology can take the heat and produce the goods for modern people. Thus theology does not feed on itself, its own history, or isolated questions, but it looks to the existential situation of modern people whom it serves as the meeting place with God.

How then does Macquarrie's method work? He begins with the existential situation. The feelings, questions, and problems that people experience become the source of the theology. The problem is brought before the believing community's tradition of teaching which opens the existential moment to the ontological reality. Finding the transparency in life that allows God to disclose both himself and his message is sought. Because no answer can be an isolated element disconnected from the entire teaching of faith, nor contradict it, the answer should be able to be related to the rest of theology. The answers of theology are then turned over to the assessment and acceptance of the believing community.

What then is Macquarrie's contribution? First, Macquarrie's method is one for all seasons. It is always relevant and contemporary. He has reminded the theological community of the power of the Word to respond to people's existential situation. Theology unlocks God's Word and often uses contemporary ways of knowing, expressing, and interpreting symbols while not displacing the revelation of God. The second is his balance. His holding relationships together is evident even in his hyphenation of existential-ontological. The balance of humanity and God, believing community and secular world, and theological answers related to other answers in a systematic wholeness add to this sense of harmony. Another word for the balance is proportionality. Macquarrie neither exaggerates questions or answers out of proportion nor does he underplay them; he asks their correct proposition. The balance gives rise to a delicacy and harmony in his theology. Tensions seem not only held together but resolved; divergences and convergences of thought when taken together yield disclosures of God and us.

Macquarrie is comprehensive and optimistic in his theology. His balance serves to translate the peace of the Gospel from intellectual interpretations into feeling tones. Yet the question of how to balance the problems given in the modern world remains. Paul Tillich stands out for his attempt to confront this very issue.

Paul Tillich

From the Enlightenment onward, the discoveries of modern science, the rise of social sciences, and the advances in historical scholarship seldom had a committed dialogue partner in Christian theology. With each holding an adversary position against the other, a great gulf seemed to form between science (reason) and religion (faith). The result was that religion and its intellectual expression in theology was regarded by the modern scientific world as a remnant left from a prescientific age which had nothing relevant to contribute. Liberal Protestant theologians like Harnack, Ritschl and Troeltsch[3] forced an entrance into this citadel and expressed the need to learn from the new developments. They tried to present another profile for theology—one concerned with modern discoveries, analysis, and problems. Liberal theology was not without its critics nor its mistakes. One critical response from within liberal theology was neo-orthodoxy. Bolstered with theologians like Barth, Brunner, H. R. Niebuhr, R. R. Niebuhr, and Bultmann, it re-emphasized the Christian message not only as open to the new advances but also as critical of them. Without doubt, liberal theology and neo-orthodoxy were pioneers of a new relationship of religion with the modern world. One of the outstanding pioneer theologians in method was Paul Tillich.

Paul Tillich, a German-born theologian who left the University of Frankfort in 1933, emigrated to the United States, and spent the remainder of his life teaching here (d. 1965), presents a theological method which tried to bring together contemporary searchings and the Christian belief. He, more than any other Protestant theologian in the twentieth century, set the example and offered a direction through his three volumes of systematic theology (completed in 1963).[4] His method of correlation has found a ready audience which has accepted, extended and developed his ideas. His influence is so pervasive among theologians of method that he continues to influence the work of many theologians at work today.

Tillich presented a method which challenged subsequent theologies to speak to the modern world. He says that method is a tool, a way around, which must be adequate to the subject matter. Adequacy cannot be judged a priori but is continually judged by its answers. No method is adequate for every subject matter, nor is it an indifferent net in which reality is caught like fish. The net is already part of reality. Method and system determine each other. Whether consciously or not, systematic theology has always used interrelation of one sort or another. Correlation means (1) the correspondence of different data, (2) logical interdependence of concepts as in polar relations (e.g. divine and human), and (3) real interdependence of things or events on structural wholes. Systematic theology proceeds from the sources, through the medium, and under the norm of Christian revelation. Answers cannot be derived from human existence alone or secularism is the result.

His method of correlation attempts to bring Christianity into dialogue with the modern world. He states that his theological system proceeds from an apologetic point of view of Christianity and carries it through in a continuous correlation with philosophy. Rather than leaving Christianity at odds with the world, he offers a vision of theology which enters the marketplace of everyday concerns. By listening to the existential questions raised, it provides its own Christian answers so that existential question and Christian answers are correlated. He prefers to see the relationships that are there mutually informing and critically enhancing each other. For example, what is the sense of Christian revelation if it applies to no one? The existential question signifies a human concern. Theology must address itself to those concerns even if they are not part of Christian revelation. Christian revelation, if it is truly for human persons, must bring meaning to the world in which we live. While Tillich's position was shocking and unusual in the 1950's it seems more natural and realistic today.[5]

Tillich prefers to think in terms of polarities which hold together divergences. Dialectics is an analytic, back-and-forth movement of yes and no. Whereas a dialectical method has a yes-no separation, he puts no such antithesis into his method. Rather than two sides of the same coin, he prefers to see them as two poles within the same field. Instead of hot and cold, he sees hot as defined by cold and cold as defined by hot. Both need the other and two perspectives become only one. By its very nature symbolization of our experience includes opposites. At one and the same time a person is thought and experience, freedom and determinism, finite and infinite, existential and essential being. To speak of freedom, for instance, is also to speak of determinism—i.e., total freedom in every facet of our lives is not ours and so we become sick and die, experience dread, anxiety, and fear. Even good requires the polarity of evil to understand it.

The polarities are not only experienced but held together also in thought. There is the polarity of the concrete and abstract, experience and thought. The two should not be confused in their functioning. If thought becomes abstract without concreteness, then people cannot understand it. And the opposite is true: concreteness without reflection leaves us in our fear, dread, and anxiety. The Christian message circles around these poles, pulled now toward one, now toward the other. In each age a different aspect of the message may dominate but the determining condition is the existential questions that are asked and responded to. Hence the doctrine of Christ at the Council of Chalcedon (451) was expressed in the fifth century in terms of their culture. The answer does not share our understanding of person and nature today and so to hold the doctrine literally is to falsify it. Hence the historicity of the questions and answers plays prominently in Tillich's method. As with his contemporary in Scripture studies Rudolf Bultmann, he understands the need to address the modern person's experience.

In the human condition, the struggle for Christian answers is one of relevancy, poignancy, and urgency. Christian answers are particularized in time and place and so must be understood as limited by their formulations and according to their contemporary situation. This limitation implies that all language, formulation, and doctrine point beyond themselves and are basically symbolic. Truth is given but never completely grasped by human terms. Theology remains open to constant change, being on-the-way, but is anchored in the revelation of Jesus Christ who is finally the Christian answer to existence. As Adam was the first creation where we all originate, Christ is the New Being where we all are directed, included, and graced. God the Father is the Ground of Being, and the sustainer of this growth into the New Being is the Spirit who makes all things new. God is our Ultimate Concern of human hopes and heartfelt cries. We are directed to him. As Christians we must have the courage to be this New Being even in the face of suffering, anxiety, persecution, or death. The cost of discipleship is the courage to be this new creation.

Christian answers illuminate existence today. Using new sciences we continue to possess new insights into the New Creation in Christ. God answers human questions and, under the impact of these answers, gives us our true identity. Theology then draws forth the questions implied in human existence and responds with the revelatory answers. Like hot and cold, questions and answers are not separated but mutually condition the other in correlation.

How does Tillich's method proceed step by step? His theology proceeds from an analysis of the situation out of which the question arises. His starting point is in the situation—"the question." Science, philosophy, and literature can help express the situation which becomes the question. Questions and answers are mutually conditioned in their polarity. Then Tillich demonstrates the symbols in the Christian message as the answers. If something is discovered which was not expected, then one must hold onto the question and reformulate the theological answer. The presupposition suggests that the substance of the answer will always be found in the revelation of Christ as the New Being.[6] While revelation is not given as a system, it is not inconsistent. Systematic theologians always try to interpret the divine reality which transcends any system. People are the questions and we are asking about ourselves and our ultimate concerns. The answers will call forth our courage to be which is the true Christian spirituality.

Tillich's contribution is his method of correlation. With it he addresses the modern world and brings theology into dialogue with it. He finds a unity between the world and grace through symbol. Theology addresses this symbol reality. He has also opened his method to answers by other religions and prepared a more ecumenical theological method. In his complete rethinking of theological symbols, artificial separations are not part of the theological enterprise. The modern world matters.

Both Tillich and Macquarrie are existentialist oriented theologians in their methods. Both resist Christian theology as having any outside-this-world starting point. Instead, like a fish swimming in a brook, sometimes in the fast current, sometimes in the pools, sometimes against the current, Christianity finds itself and its starting point always as a moving one in the flow of the contemporary situation. Existential questions locate where Christianity responds. Asking a question like how many angels fit on the head of a pin is a useless non-question. That the world around me matters is the existential starting point. Theologians then discover their starting point in human life today rather than determining it ahead of time. In this view theology is a ready responder for dialogue with the world. As a fellow traveler with the rest of humankind, theology provides from its knapsack an access to Christian revelation for everyone. Christian answers are not for an elite few but generously offered as relevant to everyone.

Existence is not a sufficient answer for either theologian. Some response of faith is needed. Macquarrie is oriented in tradition while Tillich is rooted in the interpretation of Christian tradition in modern terms. Both theologians tend to be philosophically based in existentialism. God is often treated metaphysically as the Ground of Being or Being itself. For some people the emotionally gripping description of the human situation as anxiety, alienation, and dread clashes with the intellectually abstract concept of God as Ground of Being and Ultimate Concern. For most people, the Ground of Being is not the God we worship or from whom we seek reconciliation and love. The experiential and feeling-dimension of living needs intellectual understanding too. Nevertheless the power of descriptive analysis and penetrating insight which calls forth human courage is an admirable contribution of existentialist methods.

One area that both theologians could be asked to clarify is their use of Scripture. Whenever a philosophical basis begins an analysis, at some point the revelation of Jesus Christ needs explanation. No philosophical system adequately deals with the uniqueness of Christian revelation which is based on faith. For those who continue the development of Tillich's method of correlation, for example David Tracy, interpretation of Scripture for the modern believer is addressed.

One area that Tillich especially can be challenged on is the need for Christian revelation (answers) to become a question itself. Under his method it seems that the Christian answer is not itself subject to questioning. Theology need not respond only when it has a question from the contemporary non-theological world, but it can ask a question and present itself to the world to respond. Perhaps in a leadership role or critical prophetic role, for example, love as Christ revealed it might critique the existential situation. In fact, liberation theologians will argue that the human condition is often blind and omits many concerns that need to be raised by the believer. Hence, if the rich ask the question that theology responds to, then a whole set of presuppositions will lie submerged as part of the answer. Or in other words, the question is already part of the answer. Who determines which question is more important? Consensus? Truth? Who decides? Calling the entire structural predicament into question must be done. The Christian answer must be a touchstone to assess which existential concerns are bogus or false, and which are true and grasp the real situation. Some determination and evaluation of the question itself must be made.

Another concern which is not unrelated to what has just been said is the manner of interpretation. Doing away with our negative feelings is not the answer. Perhaps pain, fear, and dread are important moments in human life that can be meaningful and not meaningless. The interpretation goes hand in hand with the explanation. Interpretation of whether an existential situation is positive or negative is open. Correctly identifying our experience will serve to provide an answer. Our next two theologians of method will address this problem.

3
Do My Experiences Count?
Empirical Method:
Tracy and Meland

In the first chapter we examined how the person encounters God today. In the second chapter we probed outward to investigate whether the world around us matters. In this third chapter we want to determine whether our experiences have meaning. Religious experience is the locus where the world and self interface. In a sense, every theology concerns itself with religious experience. Some theologians and methods place more emphasis upon it than do others. The empirical method emphasizes an experiential investigation for theology. The empirical method begins with human experience and seeks to understand the dynamic interrelationship of life. Living is comprised of inner and outer environments which contribute to the life which is lived. Without the ecological, biological, emotional, psychological, and spiritual environments, life seeps away. The empirical or experiential method examines the information of lived experience and its overlapping relationships to formulate the meaning of human life. When the encounter with God is added, the empirical method explains the meaning of life within a perspective of faith as it is experienced, not as it should be.

The adjective "American" often is synonymous with the practical or what works. This is sometimes referred to as Yankee ingenuity. No doubt that a nation had to be settled, a living fought for, and practicality was the concern. The formulation of our practicality—the philosophy of pragmatism—is one of the few distinctively American contributions to philosophy.

Experiences are not acts which a person undergoes like standing in the rain. Experiences involve the quality of presence that I exhibit in this time and place in my life. I am my experience. Experiences are my relationships to my environments of self, others, and the world. Included in my experience is the dimension of mystery which is also identified as religious experience. God is the center of this relationship. Experiences have beginnings, middles, and sometimes endings. Religious experience, i.e., coming into a relationship with God as I too grow in what life is, is in need of constant interpretation in order to foster the growth of that relationship. Understanding the relationship is what theology seeks to do. For example, the experience of God's love for me leaves me with the question of what the meaning of this love is for me. Hence the interpretation of this religious experience signifies my responsibility in the relationship. Theology seeks to clarify the meaningfulness of this experience.[1]

Our next two theologians, David Tracy and Bernard Meland, ground their theologies and consequently their methods in experience. Both have roots in the American empirical tradition and yet they are not totally empiricists, i.e., ones who hold that only experiences count. While both begin in experience, they bring experience into relationship with the faith of Christian revelation. For Tracy it will be through Christian texts; for Meland it will be through the Christian legacy. Instead of asking whether theology has anything to say to experience, these two theologians ask whether experience has anything to say to theology. The direction of their theologies moves from human experience toward the interpretation of it through two different models of experience. Tracy presents a hermeneutical model of interpretation to bear upon life experiences and Bernard Meland presents a process-relational model of the feeling-dimension which permeates religious experience. Both theologians affirm that experiences have meaning for theology.

David Tracy

Having published two significant volumes on method (*Blessed Rage for Order* in 1976 and *The Analogical Imagination* in 1981),[2] David Tracy has become an important contributor to the question of method for theology. If we were to ask him about method, he would tell us that his method emphasizes the meaningfulness of experience. An important distinction exists between meaning and meaningfulness: the former pointing to what is true (e.g., Jesus died for me) and the latter pointing to the truth as it influences my life (e.g., I live my life on the reality of Jesus' death which seals his love for me). It is not enough to say that the doctrine of Jesus Christ crucified has meaning, that is, it makes intelligent sense. Salvation is not simply a concept which makes sense, but a reality which makes an impact upon my life, makes a difference, and calls me forth to a life of commitment that is full of meaning (meaningfulness). Theology should reflect this reality. Therefore it is not enough to have religious experiences. How they affect my life is the challenge and concern. In order to answer this challenge I must interpret my experiences in the light of religious experience. Hence, for Tracy, theological method centers on the process of interpretation, called hermeneutics, whereby meaning becomes meaningfulness.

For Tracy, common human experience is the starting point for his theological vision.[3] Accepting Rahner's anthropological emphasis, that what is said about human beings also says something about God, is not enough. Experience itself brings its own dynamism. For example, every experience depends upon images, conventions, and symbolism of language as a means of communication and interpretation. We are constrained by the limits of language to express ourselves and to receive communication from others so that meaning occurs. Faith is also a part of religious experience that needs expression. The definition of theology, i.e., faith seeking understanding, acknowledges faith as a constitutive element in understanding and experience. Thus common human experience and language form a constantly changing reservoir from which understanding draws its life. Experience, if it is to be genuinely and authentically Christian, must be identified as such by the Christian community. The need for a norm by which experience is measured is found in Christian texts, especially Sacred Scriptures. Hence Tracy's method strives to correlate common human experience and language with Christian texts. Tracy's method is therefore hermeneutical and thus relies explicitly upon a process of interpretation.

Christian texts are central to the Christian tradition as classic texts. We do not have the original experience of Jesus from 30 A.D. except through the inspired writings of those who recorded it in texts or passed it down in oral tradition. Language again provides the medium for interpreted human experience. Each generation truly experiences Christ and finds Christian texts as genuinely normative for authentic Christian faith. Each person says, "This is truly my experience. Jesus is Lord." In this mutual relationship, the obverse is true as well: that Christian texts must be understood and authenticated by each generation's experience and language, place and time, challenges and contributions. Classic expressions that interpret the Christian experience emerge such as Augustine's *Confessions* or Thomas Aquinas' *Summa Theologica*. Thomas and Augustine, however, do not have the normative significance of Scripture.

Common human experience and language develop in sensitivity, depth, and meaningfulness in relation to the historical and cultural milieu. For Tracy, one need not look elsewhere for God as if God were "out there." Human experience is the realm of God's involvement with humanity and the beginning of theological reflection. God discloses himself through the common human experiences of love, joy, suffering, death, birth, reconciliation, and trust, just to mention a few. However, the revelatory manifestation varies. Imagine a series of concentric circles. Moving from the outside in, experiences can be religious, theistic, or Christian. Christianity contains the special revelatory gift of God's own Son. Thus, when a person is in love, an experience of the holy can be understood as a disclosure of God, but for the Christian it is a disclosure of the Father of Jesus and sets the seal on the veracity of Jesus' words and deeds where loving God above all and one's neighbor as one's self is the center of the Christian life.

It is not enough to experience; theologians must talk about it. While any verbalization of an experience is difficult, imperfect, and incomplete, nevertheless language remains an important medium of interpretation. As symbolic, personal and social language communicates much more than words. A person, for example, might not have the same identical experience of suffering but he or she does know what it means to suffer and can understand another's pain, anguish, sacrifice, frustration, and fear. Hence, I might not know what it means to die of cancer but I do know what it means to suffer and to sit with another person as he or she lies dying and involves me with the struggle, pain, and release from biological life. I cannot pretend to have had the same experience, but the identical one is not necessary, because the meaning of suffering is communicated to me.

While sitting with another person who is dying of cancer is a virtuous Christian act, it does not constitute theology. Even to verbalize common human experience is not theology. To bring the Christian faith to bear upon the meaning of suffering is theology. While not exhausting the interpretation, Christian texts serve as the norm for all Christian interpretations. The theological challenge becomes the critical correlating of both common human experience and language with Christian texts in mutual relation. Perhaps the result will be a fresh expression of the Christian life today.

One important theological factor that Tracy nicely includes in his theology is the retrieval of tradition. Christian tradition is a rich deposit of experience, wisdom, and theology that can help faith today. Retrieval implies that I do not live in the year 30 and I do not experience my life situation the same way people then did. However, a continuity of experience whereby I encounter the risen Lord does continue and is woven through human history. Thus theology should help dispose me to the Christian experience and allow me to recognize God's active communication with my experiences today.

Tracy tells us how to critically correlate common human experience and language with Christian texts. On the side of common human experience, he prefers a phenomenological analysis of the religious dimension of human experience. One need not be a Christian to investigate this dimension. Everyday language and scientific explanations can help explain what is happening. With respect to the second source, Christian texts, historical and hermeneutical investigation are the principles of investigation.

Tracy describes five fundamental methods of doing theology which are part of the Christian tradition.[4] An examination of them by their claims to truth, strengths and weaknesses will shed light upon his own method.

The first model is the Orthodox model. Claims made by the modern world do not necessarily have any inner-theological relevance. The task of theology described at Vatican I (1879–80) is a clear example where theology functions as a proof to support beliefs. The task of the theologian is an adequate understanding of the beliefs of his or her particular church tradition. The strength of this model is that it concerns itself with what faith says. It develops sophisticated models of belief within a church with no contact with other disciplines or claims. The weakness is that revelation overrides all other considerations and needs no help for interpretation.

The second model is the liberal model which accepts the ethical and existential commitment to secular faith as a constitutive drive present in all modern science as the heart of the liberal enterprise. Liberal theologians find themselves committed to the values of modern experiments, namely free and open inquiry, autonomous judgments, critical investigation of all claims to truth. The strength of this model is that it dialogues with the modern world's disciplines (sciences, technology, philosophy, etc.) but its weakness lies in its inadequacies of the conclusions where so much is mixed together. Examples of this model are the Catholic modernists like Loisy and the Protestant liberals like Schleiermacher and Harnack.

The third model is the neo-orthodox model which continues the liberal tradition and is not really a new alternative but rather a moment within a larger liberal tradition. Committed to the liberal analysis of the human situation, the neo-orthodox theologian insists that the negative elements of sin, tragedy, and suffering are unaccounted for. The unique gift of faith is needed. This model's strength is its radical faith in the God of Jesus Christ. Its weakness lies in its inability to take the modern world's contribution as part of that experience. Examples of this model are Tillich and Barth as well as Rahner and liberation theologians.

The fourth model is the radical theology model of whom the "death of God" theologians are a primary instance (Altizer, Hamilton, van Buren). It insists that the God of the liberal, neo-orthodox, and orthodox theologians alienates the authentic conscience of the liberated contemporary human being. Their God must die in order for the human to live. This model's strength is its ability to pinpoint the question of the traditional understanding of the Christian God. Its weakness is its inability to judge the special character of revelation and affirm the reality of God. The question arises then whether under this model one can really continue the Christian enterprise.

The fifth model is the revisionist model which is committed to the dramatic confrontation, the mutual illumination and correction, the possible basic reconciliation between principles of values, cognitive claims, and existential faith of both reinterpreted post-modern consciousness and reinterpreted Christianity. The most obvious examples of this model are the process theologians. The other four models make a contribution but are judged inadequate for the present modern world and what it accepts and knows. There is a need in the modern world to continue the critical task of faith by historical, philosophical, and social scientific research and reflection. The task is the dramatic confrontation between modern consciousness and reinterpreted Christianity. The revisionist model holds the experience of the past in critical correlation with Christian texts in order to interpret the meaningfulness of the religious experience today.

Within the revisionist model, theology can be subdivided into three parts: foundational (i.e., coming to believe), systematics (i.e., organizing and clarifying the beliefs), and practical (i.e., the application of beliefs in practice). At present Tracy has written two volumes which treat respectively of foundational and systematic theology. When completed, the third volume will allow his method to be discussed as an integrated whole. While the completion is eagerly awaited, Tracy's hermeneutical insights have greatly contributed to the contemporary development of theology.

Religious experience is not an easily agreed upon topic of interpretation. Tracy examines the process at work in coming to believe which is his foundational theology. Common human experience that becomes religious is the first layer. The divine is understood as the holy, the other, the one beyond, the powerful one. The experience of the holy comes in moments of birth and death, love and creation. Religion is not necessary to interpret it. But is this all? According to Tracy, religious experience in its thematized, or explicitated, understanding yields the concept of God. The God-experience (theistic as opposed to religious) identifies and interprets divine mystery. Buddhists, Moslems, and Hindus share this thematized understanding of God. Just as God is a revelation of the holy, so too is Jesus Christ a special revelation of God. Likewise, just as revelation manifests a God within a religious experience, so too does the Christ revelation exhibit a special revelation within the experience of God. Because the fullest revelation of God is in Christ, all religious experience points to and is summed up by Christ even if people do not know him. Christianity's responsibility in theology is the continued clarity, dialogue, and preaching of the Christ revelation for all. Everyone need not become a Christian. But Christianity specifies the search of the human community for the meaning of God. Hence Christians should dialogue with other religions and non-religions recognizing that belief, whether religious or theistic, may have much in common from which all can benefit. The very same God of Jesus acts in each case.

Our second question can now be raised: How does Tracy's method proceed? Every interpretation must include within it the two principles of coherency and adequacy. As the many religions testify, many interpretations of religious experience are possible. The principle of coherency asks whether the criteria of the experience holds together through the explanation. The principle of adequacy asks whether the criterion of the experience has been sufficiently responded to by the explanation. The principle of coherency which asks whether the explanation makes sense is a question regarding truth (meaning); the principle of adequacy which asks whether the explanation interprets the data sufficiently is a question regarding acceptability (meaningfulness). Foundational theology is concerned with the truth-claim and addresses other disciplines represented by the academy. Systematic theology is concerned with the truth-bearing character of religious tradition and is hermeneutical in character, especially the analogical imagination. Practical theology is concerned with that analysis of some radical situation of ethical-religious import (e.g., sexism, racism, economic exploitation). The notion of truth in practical theology is transformational, i.e., living the commitment of the Gospel tests one's acceptance of truth.

Theology does not hold on for dear life to neat and clean answers but for dear love to whether there is integrity in the seeking of truth for human life. Explanations seem to be a dime a dozen but correct interpretations are a rarer purchase. Theological method is an art needing skill, sensitivity, knowledge, and openness to allow others to confirm or deny the interpretation. Tracy talks about three areas of responsibility for every theologian: to the Church, the academy, and society.[5] Every theologian must allow the members who share the faith, i.e., forming a Church, the opportunity to judge the work. The academy of different disciplines (whether social, scientific, aesthetic) must also be allowed to contribute to and argue about the intellectual integrity of the interpretation. Finally, the society of all people whether believers or not for whom every religious statement belongs must argue and judge what is human. A theology which only talks to other theologies misses its constituency as do theologians who only talk to like-minded supporters who, at the extreme, form elite groups or cults. The Christian message proclaims that God has revealed that salvation is for all people. Theology needs to address the various audiences of the human family.

What is Tracy's contribution to theological method? Tracy shares similarities with Rahner and Lonergan. While he also insists upon an anthropological beginning, he emphasizes the importance of religious experience both as a source for doing theology and as an end product of theological reflection. Rahner and Lonergan prefer knowledge as an opening to God. Tracy's decidedly clear use of Scripture and principles of application for interpretation are clearer than the others. With each theological method we recognize a clearer dependency upon and use of Scripture which is due in part to the recent advances in Scripture study. Tracy not only uses Scripture but also goes a step farther in the hermeneutical application of the principles of interpretation. In what is a new twist to the empirical method, experience becomes the ground where Scripture is planted and rooted. Like Rahner and Lonergan, Tracy stresses human response to God's invitation and is incarnational in his theology.

Whereas Lonergan has a complete system of theology based upon the functional specialties of the act of understanding, Tracy builds a complete system from common human experience and language. Tracy's method appears wider in scope than Lonergan's in that it can be tapped into on more levels than understanding. Also, whereas Lonergan's method is invariant about the way the mind operates, Tracy's method addresses a closer cooperation between thinking and action in the form of interpretation to inform foundational and systematic theology. If it can be said that Lonergan prefers the context of the mind, then Tracy can be said to prefer the context of human experience.

Whereas Rahner is concerned with religious experience as it opens the person to knowledge and freedom, Tracy opens the religious experience itself to Christian texts. Interpretation with its retrieval of the history of the experience of God's revelation in Christ constantly norms theology. At times it seems that the shifts are subtle but these little differences trigger major differences in results.

Tracy's major contribution is the central place of religious experience and the pastoral application of the method. His use of hermeneutical principles emphasizes an important relationship of experience and Scripture held together through the retrieval of tradition.

One could argue whether or not Tracy relies too heavily upon the written word. His use of symbols and the analogical imagination does not penetrate the feeling dimension of religious experience to sufficiently render them a true and adequate part of theology. Our next theologian, Bernard E. Meland, also uses the empirical method but capitalizes upon the feeling dimension as an integral factor for doing theology.

Bernard E. Meland

The hermeneutical work of David Tracy, especially his emphasis upon language, provides an appropriate context for understanding our next theologian who has written in the area of empirical theology for more than fifty years. Bernard E. Meland (1899–   ) prefers to emphasize symbols as the expression of reality that we experience. Consequently, the meaningfulness of religious experience cannot ignore the feeling-dimension of reality that conditions our understanding and puts it in context. In 1976 Meland finished the third volume of his trilogy on Christian faith, *Fallible Forms and Symbols*,[6] which specifically addresses the question of method. He also complements Tracy's revisionist theology.

Meland is considered a process theologian. More correctly, he draws upon the American philosophical resources of William James and Alfred North Whitehead. Meland does not purchase their philosophical insights wholesale. By including faith in relation to Whitehead's philosophy of organism, he critically examines the role of faith in relation to contemporary scientific thinking. Instead of the word "process," which emphasizes only one aspect of his thought, some prefer to describe Meland's theology as "process-relational" in order to emphasize its organic and contextual aspects. His method examines process and development but within the web of relationships that make up a context. Meland is often regarded as a cultural theologian because of his insistence upon the relationships involved in experience. It is from this insistence upon relationships that he presents experience as richer, deeper, and thicker than the conceptual clarification of it that language represents. Moreover he stresses that our feelings include "feelings of tendency" (James) or a sense of the direction events are flowing (Whitehead calls these prehensions). For example, the politician searches for the direction that voters are going in order to set a platform. Within theology the question becomes how one deals with this feeling-dimension in experience. Although language must be employed to express feelings, symbol rather than language conveys the true theological beginning point. The term sacrament expresses for some theologians the overarching category of symbol.[7]

If we were to ask Meland about theological method, he would tell us that the context of doing theology is more important than our other theologians have so far indicated. Although every theologian has at least indirectly spoken about religious experience, none, not even Tillich, more consciously explores the interrelationship of religious experience to the cultural symbols which mediate it to individuals. Culture is like a stream that carries down the preserved values, ideas, feelings, institutions, furnishings, and symbols of the past to the present. Human beings live in and through culture as the ambient from which we grow and draw resources for growth. Culture has a dynamism of its own and like the stream exhibits power on the rise or on the decline. Theology floats and interacts with these dynamics. For example, with the rise of Scripture scholarship in the last half century, the scriptural dimensions of theology are now actively explored in every discipline. Yet the cultural dynamism extends farther than that. For example we can walk into the twelfth century Chartres Cathedral and be overwhelmed with its witness to faith in the twentieth century. Perhaps, and most likely, it is not the identically same experience of those who experienced it in the twelfth century. Nevertheless there is a clear witness to faith which remains constant in its symbolism to faith. Through human choice, culture brings values forward in different forms and through varied symbols. However, the symbols are not always clear to the one experiencing them and thus a fallibility exists with them as they are caught up in their own history and interpretations.

As praiseworthy and necessary as any analysis of culture would be, this is not Meland's purpose. God works through culture and the relationships that bind me to my context. Thus even today I can undergo a conversion at Chartres, become more aware of God walking the city streets, and praise him for his dealings with me. Hence my interrelationships beyond myself that extend to other persons and events remain fundamental to my religious experience.

No one is an island in this theology. If one presses beneath the surface of the water, one finds that below the surface we are all connected by land. Life depends upon a series of relationships beginning with the biological level and continuing through the emotional, psychological, social, and spiritual levels. Whitehead, for one, tried to present a view of life taking into account this organic and dynamic set of relationships. Life is connected relationally and developmentally. He referred to it as a philosophy of organism; others called it a process theology. Meland shares Whitehead's organic, processive, and relational perspective.

Since culture is mediated through symbols, our intellect must be able to know and act from what is presented. The human person is the key that unlocks the world. The human person possesses not only the power of rational consciousness but also the power of appreciative and ethical consciousnesses as well. For example, Chartres Cathedral is not a text which I can read, and yet, in stone and glass, it speaks more eloquently about the holiness of God than an explanation. Overtaken by wonder, I am emotionally moved and intellectually drawn into the experience so that an openness of mind and heart toward God's majesty occurs. In turn this experience becomes part of my life, my history from which I live, and I reflect on the meaningfulness of my own life. I can never re-create the experience itself when I talk to people back in the United States, but I do believe even more in God's love and discern feelings about the direction of my life. I feel responsible to God, myself, and others. This movement in myself to authenticity and responsibility is processive. Hence symbols grab me outwardly, drive inwardly, and lead me forward to live my life. Encounters with symbols that focus my life require organic, processive and relational responses of my total self. Responsive awareness is necessary to become genuinely human.

Clarity of thought, Meland reminds us, is not necessarily the same as clarity of truth. For example, in physics, to speak about the plum pudding model of the atom may be clear, even adequately explain electrons and protons as random plums mixed in the pudding, and allow for new exploration of the data, but the model is not truth even though it discloses something of the truth. Nuclear physics eventually discarded this model entirely in favor of a planetary model. In theology, for example, dividing the Trinity into its economic and immanent relations might be clear, but the experience of the triune God in love remains the richer, deeper, and not as clear experience. Like one who is in love and finds words inadequate to explain the experience of love, reality resists any definitive, final explanations. Similarly, for any deeply human experience of which religious experience is one, clear words do not capture the experience. When clarification takes place through the medium of language, Meland reminds us not to discard the richness and truth of the feeling-dimension inherent in the experience.

The basic presupposition for Meland can be succinctly stated that reality is deeper, richer, and fuller than any concept or expression and cannot be reduced to a concept. This statement does not imply that the truth is not approximately known in the clarification process. For instance a mother cannot explain her love for her child but she knows it is there and lives her life by it. Or, two lovers both know that something is wrong between them by subtle and unspoken communications in silence and eye contact. Trusting the feeling of tendency is important both for the lovers and for the mother who base their lives upon it. While further clarification is sought after to check out the feeling, in the meantime personal relationships, decisions, and evaluations grow or diminish because of it.

Meland suggests an understanding of faith that stretches beyond the explanations of reason to our feeling about the context wherein we reside. God is present both in the individual and in the context. Hence Meland interrelates what we know through rational thinking with what we know through non-rational understanding, i.e., the kind of knowledge which comes from sensitivity, beauty, fittingness, and love.

Meland's insight is his interrelating of the appreciative and rational consciousnesses. To leave out the rational would be to sink into the well of emotionalism. To leave out the appreciative would be to soar into the heights of rationalism. True theology must examine experience where feeling is part of thinking and thinking a part of feeling.

It is of little wonder then that Meland's process-relational method emphasizes the role of the context, especially culture. The human being cannot be extricated from the contextual relationships of physical environment, business, economics, society, history, the community, or the self. This would be tantamount to taking a redwood tree out of the forest and into a laboratory, or a child away from its mother and father. The web of the world's relationships reflects humanity as increasingly intertwined, interconnected, and inescapably involved. God works through this web of relationships. Meland calls the distinctive empirical activity of God, which creates newness from the past, connects itself with me, and draws me forward, the Creative Passage.[8] Meland emphasizes not simply the process-relational aspect but also the transformational aspect through connectedness with God in faith. Through our free choice we cooperate with God and participate in his life through and in this world. The organic process of involved love with God is an interchange that is creative and transforms the web of relationships into a qualitative relation of love. Through faith we penetrate the superficiality of the world as a string of islands to recognize God working and being actively present uniting us below the surface. All reality whether suffering, joy, gentleness, or love becomes a source for finding God. In this view God is not set over and against science, the world, or people but, on the contrary, dwells with and in them. While God is present to us, the symbols and expressions themselves are not to be mistaken for God himself. Likewise we must not forget that the experience of God is not God himself.

Within the Christian experience, Meland identifies three levels of witness to faith which exist and exhibit a constant contact for what is distinctively Christian.[9] The first is the individual and other individuals who are Christian believers. From their faith one discovers a developing faith that resembles mine and where I can identify God working and encountering me. The second is in the culture. I am in this with others. Culture discloses God working and encountering me through events, structures, values, and the past. I am in this through symbols, values, institutions, and structures. The third is the Christian legacy, most especially the Scriptures but also the faith handed down through hundreds of years of believing. I am in this with believers who have left a legacy for my benefit. The Christian legacy holds an authoritative expression of the past in the way faith was lived because of its revelatory nature. As dynamically interrelated these three witnesses of faith have both a content and a direction. Thus one has a feeling for the organic growth that these three witnesses testify to. Turning oneself sensitively to the invisible movement of God results in my own increased openness, receptivity, and participation. Spiritually holy people possess a sensitivity of this type which finds God's movement and presence wherever it is. Neat and clean lines that fence God in and restrict his salvific design are not what Meland seeks. He prefers an expansive vision which finds him wherever he leads.

How then does Meland's method proceed step by step? First of all, Meland introduces the appreciative awareness as a necessary skill in examining the empirical data of religious experience. Appreciative awareness begins in open awareness to the context itself. One must not prejudice the event which screens God's self-communication to me. Only a willingness to encounter what is there allows reality to enter as unprejudiced message. While pure objectivity is not something that we can attain, neither can we, with jaundiced vision, enter an encounter with our minds already made up. Removing the filters that screen out reality is the first task. Wonder is the characteristic of this first step.[10]

The second step is identification. What enters into open awareness comes into relation with consciousness. The perceiving mind receives the communicated meaning but does not stop to analytically think about it. Like someone listening to music, the rhythm, instruments, tone, and volume are perceived while listening and no dissection occurs at the time. The whole person attends the symphony, or encounter, and is acutely aware of what is going on while being pulled by the musical event. Empathy is the characteristic of this second step.

The third step is discrimination. This step stops to formally analyze what is going on. The quantitative and qualitative features of the event are examined within the context itself, or the total experience. It differentiates the datum into a distinctive event. One might say that the symphony, for example, was good because it correctly rendered the music and performed it in an inspiring way. Thus the person is critically developing his or her musical appreciation in relation to the event and will be able to become a music appreciator. Of course, study and talking to others will help correct and hone this person's appreciative skills.

Once the appreciative awareness is put in place, and it is the key to Meland's explanation of religious experience, the person brings his or her faith experience to bear upon the finding of the Creative Passage actively working in the world. Feeling of tendency, a goodness not our own, freedom and joy, all become a blended part of living. Life becomes an art rather than a syllogism. Faith now empowers the individual to hear God speaking through the world. Understanding becomes appreciating God's ways with us and responding accordingly. It is little wonder that Meland refers to his appreciative awareness as "responsive awareness." Yet this is not one-sided. Mutual interaction is called for. Love strives to love more, faith to believe more, and hope to hope more. Who can pray for long years without being called to more trust and love? Other individuals, the culture, and the Christian legacy inspire and direct us with the norms for finding God's presence with us. The feeling-dimension of religious experience truly yields a knowledge of God that I live by. Reason's understanding of it helps me to clarify what is going on, articulate my feelings, but never does substitute for them. Reason serves to clarify my entire attitude, emotions, context and my response to them in order to aid my fuller participation and life in God within the world.

Meland is a theologian of religious experience who takes feeling seriously. Faith is no less real in the feeling-dimension of an event. Love has a knowledge that it communicates only to those in love. Lovers need no explanations. Like dancers they move to the music of love. No one can objectify a loving touch or embrace—it is irreducible to rational explanations. Yet we all live in the glow of joy and goodness that is communicated and base our ethical decisions upon it even if we do not totally understand it. We know the love, and that is directive for my response. Theology, as a clarifying and reflective process that seeks understanding, cannot overstep the data provided by faith in the feeling-dimension of living. Once theology comes to an explanation it cannot forget the feelings of the original experience. Thomas a Kempis' famous phrase contained the truth of this problem when he said that he would rather feel compunction than be able to define it. Love, therefore, can never become a proposition but must be kept alive in the feelings. Meland is a theologian of the entire experience and the entire person.

What has Meland contributed to method? Meland and Tracy represent two theologians who emphasize the meaningfulness of religious experience along with its meaning. They have widened the notion of experience and have taken its demands seriously. For Tracy the clarification of theological truths depends upon the interpretation of common human experience and language critically correlated with Christian texts. For Meland theological truth remains wider than narrow explanations and rests in the richness of cultural symbols which are experienced and grasped by the feeling-dimension. The richness of liturgy, prayer, sacraments, and devotions supports and conveys theological truth through a sensitivity for God. The theological maxim is the law of prayer is the law of belief *(lex orandi, lex credendi)*. Meland challenges any theological method which works out concepts while neglecting the data of the feelings.

While Tracy works on a hermeneutics of experience and text which is linguistically oriented, Meland works on a hermeneutics of contextual feeling and symbolic forms. For God meets us not only in the deepest centers of our selves but also in the farthest galaxy, even though we will travel there only in the future.

For Meland, Rahner's description of the human person as the Hearer of the Word is transformed to a conversation partner with the Lord of the Creative Passage where gestures, tones, textures, and silences are part of the language. Lonergan's notion of conversion extends the appreciative dimension beyond the individual to a conversion toward the world in a type of political conversion. Meland offers an interchange with culture that is pragmatically oriented where one finds the Kingdom of God by the creative interchange with God. More than any other theologian we will meet, Meland is the champion of the aesthetic, the cultural context, and feeling-dimension. Life as art, as symbolic, as sacramental emphasizes the truth found in the beauty of God and humankind. No method can ignore or forget this feeling-dimension.

4
Can I Find God in Suffering?
Socio-Phenomenological Method:
Schillebeeckx and Sobrino

The term "culture" appeared for the first time as a Catholic theological concept at the Second Vatican Council (1962–65). The Constitution on the Church in the Modern World *(Gaudium et Spes)* used it to designate the social, political, and economic context of the world. The result is that the Church must examine its relationship with culture. Within different cultures, since the world has no one culture, different values compete. One example is a capitalist state vs. a communist state. The growing acceptance of the term culture as an overarching concept signals theologians of method to examine it formally. Two such theologians begin with the cultural situation of the modern world to develop their respective theologies. The methods are socio-phenomenological because they begin in a phenomenological and social analysis of the society and individual. The first is presented by the Dutch Dominican Edward Schillebeeckx and the second by the Salvadorean Jesuit liberation theologian Jon Sobrino. Their analysis begins in the human cry made throughout the world: Can God be found in suffering? From two different geographical areas of the world, two different hemispheres, from the first and the third world countries, this same question is asked. As might not be expected, the same answer but from two different viewpoints is offered. Never before has the theological community been so geographically widespread yet so ideologically close. A theology which is inculturated and yet which crosses cultural boundaries is forming. We are witnessing a new kind of theology in the making.

Edward Schillebeeckx

Schillebeeckx has recently written two volumes of a projected triology (*Jesus* in 1974, and *Christ* in 1977)[1] in which he develops a new theology that speaks to the world situation today. I use the word "new" because, as one of the important theologians of Vatican II, he sketches a theology in harmony with the concerns expressed in the document on the Church in the Modern World. Schillebeeckx represents an increasing number of theologians who speak both to Catholics and also to the wider audience of all Christians and anyone who will listen. From the insistence of Vatican II to move the Church out into the modern world, Catholic theology cannot be a ghetto theology. This reach extends outward and distinctively marks a way of doing theology responsible to all humanity. Since it is open for all, its scope includes a beginning point that people of good will can accept and is shared by others. Such a beginning point need not rest upon revelation, but instead a phenomenological acceptance of the world situation that leads to revelation will suffice. Therefore whether one is Hindu, Buddhist, or atheist, anyone can enter into dialogue with Schillebeeckx.

While it is true that all can enter the dialogue, some may not continue with it. At some stage in the discussion the revelation of Jesus Christ enters and may require faith in order to continue the dialogue. Hence the dialogue may simultaneously speak both to people outside the Church (i.e., an invitation to anyone seeking truth) and to people inside the Church (i.e., people committed to Christian faith as a truth). Because of this dual function, which is truly a difference in style from pre-Vatican II theologies, misinterpretation of both theologians and theologies can occur. Schillebeeckx, Rahner, and Küng are only a few examples of theologians whose objectives have sometimes been misunderstood. Nevertheless we are entering into a new way of doing theology for many audiences that we must learn from and whose primary characteristic is a deeper insertion of the believer into the modern world.

Schillebeeckx founds his theology on the experience of suffering humanity.[2] While suffering can be a salutary act (e.g., birthing a child, the cost of love, the price of commitment) there exists useless suffering (e.g., starvation, oppression, hatred, violence). While the former can be humanizing the latter is dehumanizing and bears no apparent salvific quality. Salvation of humanity in Jesus cannot reconcile dehumanization. It must be resisted, rejected, and refused. No matter what religious or nonreligious belief one has chosen, atheist, Buddhist, Christian, etc., all agree on the dehumanizing character of suffering and the need to eradicate it.

If theology, and therefore the revelation of Jesus, will be relevant to the modern world, then it must speak to the modern world of a salvation that is needed. Since the concept of salvation often seems removed from us as an eternal rest in heaven, it is usually not important to the suffering humanity today unless it is an opium that drugs the people away from the pain. From the European culture where the battle of belief and unbelief rages, the answer of belief cannot lose sight of its Christ-given message that all are called to salvation. Hence it must have an immediate impact in our day. The transformation of the world and not just belief is at stake. Salvation is not just a concept but a commitment to act and transform the unjust structures that dehumanize us. The human reality is that if some are dehumanized then we all are dehumanized.

Suffering is a negative experience that all people can agree needs elimination. For those with a religious belief, all world religions specifically address suffering. Thus whether one possesses a religious belief or not, a common human starting point exists for dialogue about God, humanity, and salvation. As the dialogue proceeds, the reasons why each religion is motivated to eliminate suffering will differ according to the revelations of each. For example, Hindus motivate themselves by seeing suffering as an illusion, Buddhists by identifying themselves with Buddha's compassion, Moslems by the brotherhood of all believers, and so on. The Christian holds an understanding of suffering based on the revelation of Christ and must remain faithful to that tradition. This fidelity brings up the question of the interpretation of the experience of Jesus as Lord which is what theology treats. Preeminently the Jesus experience is discovered in Scripture but it exists no less in the experienced world of grace today. Christian experience today is interpreted by Scripture. The role of theology is to express the understanding of this Christian revelation today.

Before moving into Schillebeeckx's understanding of the interpretation of the Jesus experience, notice that he does not let the conversation about how to do theology stop the obligation to love God and neighbor. Salvation is a performative concept, i.e., one that must not simply be talked about but acted upon. Theology's role of clarifying the understanding of faith should not block or detract from the fundamental obligation to live the Gospel. In living the Gospel a knowledge results that nourishes faith. Thus Schillebeeckx calls for a recognition of the underlying interrelationship of religious experience which unites knowledge and action. When action and thought work together one informs the other. Even in the face of intellectual uncertainties, one does not stop living the faith. Nor in the face of lived uncertainties does one stop living the faith that seeks understanding. Theology is not like icing on the cake; it emerges from what we are as human people.[3]

One other observation needs to be made. Schillebeeckx begins from what he calls a "negative viewpoint." This means that by looking at the absurdity of suffering (negative) a commitment to do something about it results (positive). One might take note that the commitment is emotionally motivated. This negative dialectic contains the additional capacity to define something about salvation: i.e., minimally salvation implies the humanization of the world by the eradication of suffering. While a Christian shares this minimal commitment, by revelation he or she is committed to a maximal understanding of salvation described in terms of love of God and neighbor even to the apparently extreme absurdity of loving an enemy. Salvation then extends across a whole spectrum of what it means to be human even though room exists for different religious viewpoints. By its revelatory experience, Christianity commits itself to the minimal as well as the maximal interpretations as found and given in Christ's own suffering and death. Hence, rather than a dual commitment, for the Christian it is the very same one.

How does Schillebeeckx use his method? Beginning from a phenomenological examination of suffering, he presents the interpretation of the experience of Jesus as Lord. But a correct interpretation is not easy nor universally accepted. The norm of the experience of Jesus, or what we use even today to identify our experiences as a Christian experience of faith, exists in the New Testament, specifically the Gospels. Interpreting a first century document presents problems of its own both from a twentieth century mentality and from a radically different cultural context. Thus the meaning of the early Christian context from which the images, language, and presuppositions were drawn and commonly held must be opened up. In every culture values not expressed lurk like shadows behind everything that is illuminated in speech. Often what is not said is as important as what is said. It is important therefore not only to know what the words of Scripture mean but also what presuppositions, images, and concerns existed in the minds of the authors and audience in that culture.

Schillebeeckx sets out to examine not only the words of Scripture but also the cultural context which conditions them. The bridging of first century and twentieth century in terms of culture is rather new to theological method. The critical scholarly tools are there to be used thanks to more than a century of historical and critical scholarship. But the time has come when these findings widen the context for a better understanding of the times themselves. It would be fair to say that we know more in the twentieth century about the first century than others did in any previous century. Archeological findings like the Dead Sea Scrolls, scientific methods of dating and preserving material, infra-red reproductions of tablets and scrolls, and linguistic development are only a few of the ways that we can examine the Scriptures and know about former times.

Specifically, for Schillebeeckx, the authors of the Synoptic Gospels (Matthew, Mark, and Luke) wrote about different themes according to their experience of Jesus as Lord. As a gradual written tradition emerged, a richer theological reflection occurred. John and Paul differ from the Synoptic writers because they understood the experience of Jesus in slightly nuanced ways and expressed this to totally different audiences of believers. If the cultural conditioning of Scripture is not understood, then the Christ experience for me might be wrongly interpreted and forced into a twentieth century mentality where, through misinterpretation, non-essentials could masquerade as essentials. For example, Paul's admonition to the women of Corinth to cover their heads lest it be interpreted as a sign of licentiousness has little to do today with a sign of orthodoxy. Using Paul this way is to misinterpret the implications of faith today.

Once the relationship of Christian revelation in relation to its cultural conditioning is examined, then the revelation can be moved forward so to speak into the twentieth century. The continuity of the experience of Christ can be allowed to take form in the new and present day cultural context. The challenge of the Gospels is to live authentic discipleship in our place and time, in our cultural demands. Christ did not speak about nuclear war, for instance, yet we as Christians must address this situation today in fidelity to who we are as revealed by Christ. This living out of our life becomes the way of experiencing Jesus as Lord today. For those who eradicate the suffering of starvation, oppression, hatred, etc. know in their hearts the meaning of salvation and God's commitment to us.[4]

God is experienced in the immediacy or present moment of such apparently worldly work. Schillebeeckx sums up God's grace permeating the world and calling us forth to respond in Christian faith as "mediated immediacy."[5] The world is grace yet it is recognized, or mediated, through the present immediacy of our encountering experience of God. God is immediately and salvifically present in our attempts at humanization and at the same time he resists our acts of dehumanization. Even a medical discovery of penicillin which alleviates futile suffering and thus brings humanization is none other than an act of grace.

What is Schillebeeckx's contribution? While his third volume awaits completion and can possibly make further contributions, nevertheless he has made several already. First, by starting with suffering, his method is remarkably ecumenical. He invites everyone of good will to enter into dialogue with the Christian message. Second, although he uses Scripture as normative, he insists on an interpretation which varies from culture to culture. He has demonstrated that historical-critical method does not stand alone in its ability to interpret the Christian experience. It needs historical-critical scholarship evaluated in a particular culture and the historical development of the faith until the present which is the work of systematic theology. For example, the message of Jesus is a biblical question that requires the interpretation of Scripture. The answer to that question is not the end of the search. What meaning and implication it has for me today goes beyond the biblical question. We do not disregard the two thousand years of Christian experience. Hence Schillebeeckx argues for the cooperation of all areas of theology in addressing, understanding, and expressing the meaning of Jesus as Lord. What was a wave of biblical results in scholarship is only one essential step in a whole process that must bring to bear upon the modern world the Christian experience.

The third contribution is his emphasis upon the performative nature of salvation: overturn the dehumanizing processes by living a committed life in Christ. As one lives the faith, the Holy Spirit meets us and opens us up to God's life. The faith that theology serves must finally be lived, and in living do we learn of the Lord's ways.

While Schillebeeckx treats suffering as a starting point for theology, he lacks the specific identification of the causes of evil. Our next theologian will identify dehumanization as it occurs in the large structural evils which cause suffering and oppression. More than Schillebeeckx, the next theologian recognizes and wrestles with specific inculturated problems.

Jon Sobrino

Another theological method that begins its reflection from the cultural context of humanity is Latin American liberation theology. The self-designated liberation theologians are a wave of European-trained scholars who returned to Latin America only to discover that European based theology had little relevance to their cultural situation. A conceptual framework stamped itself upon the cultural situation from the top so to speak and thereby failed to express their "grassroots" faith.

As part of the culturally-minded theologians of a post-Vatican II Church, these theologians recognized that European theology dominated but its primary focus on faith and unbelief did not apply in their Catholic dominated countries where belief was not questioned. Gradually with the emergence of fine Latin American theologians, the vibrant revolutionary cries of the heart clashed with the slow evolutionary ideas of the mind. The result was cataclysmic.

The growing social discrepancy between rich and poor, the political oppression and control of decision-making policies, and economic dependency, which through victimization by other countries and multinational powers dictated internal procedures, compounded the volatile situation that cried out for liberation. A hallowed Gospel of love that is preached but does not also bring a removal of oppression and unjust structures is a hollow one. For instance, the Kingdom of God that Jesus preached brought actual changes to the poor, oppressed, marginal and sinners. In Latin America, the Gospel seemed to be a tool for maintaining the status quo politically, economically, and socially. Marx's famous reference to religion as an opium for the people was not lost upon the people of Latin America. Here religion becomes the doctor and accuses the macro-structure of the socio-politico-economic order of being a new drug. Violence, suffering, and oppression are the effects of this drug. Religion itself suffers from these residual effects. Before the Gospel can take root in people's hearts, the dehumanizing conditions must be reversed. Any cooperation with the continuing evolution is tantamount to allowing evil to continue unchecked. This brand of theology calls for a liberation of oppression and oppressed peoples in every sense of the word, particularly in the macro-structures of evil which dominate this culture.

In the recent decades great advances have occurred in our understanding of the macro-structures of society, politics, and economics. The laws which govern these structures are now more accessible to human analysis. Also, humanity can now control these laws and take a more determinative role in the directing of them. However, the power to control these laws resides in the hands of a powerful and elite few. Participation in the direction of society and its subsequent self-determination does not belong to the society in general. Instead, strings are pulled from every part of the globe with the exception of the people within the situation. When the people ask for their rights to land, trade, self-determination, and participation in the world's process, oppressive powers act against these internal requests.

The situation exists not only in Latin America but, by definition, in every so-called third world country as well. These underdeveloped and dependent countries seem historically condemned through no fault of their own to maintain their status quo just to survive. The pain expressed by liberation theologians who find themselves and the majority of their people alienated from their own land is too raw and real. The plaintive cry of frustration and powerlessness breeds an anger that has been echoed and re-echoed from the Americas to Southeast Asia, to Africa.[6]

Particularly sensitized by these theologians, the church in Latin America took a radical step by identifying themselves with the plight of the poor and oppressed. Despite bloodshed, reprisals, and threats of punishment against the church, this courageous stance on behalf of the people and Gospel stayed its course.

Because the situation is volatile and theologians themselves are silenced and harassed, the work of liberation theology advances in fits and starts. However, they have already made a substantial mark on theology: that the socio-politico-economic context within a culture is necessary for theological reflection on faith.

The Salvadorean Jesuit Jon Sobrino has written one of the few Latin American Christologies (*Christology at the Crossroads,*[7] 1976). In it he sketches out the method for doing theology in a liberation context. Although he admits that it is not complete and needs more analysis, his program is truly representative of this theology and Sobrino remains an important contributor. In the beginning of the movement, liberation theologians found kindred expressions of the need for deliverance from Exodus and the dramatic Old Testament denunciations of social injustice. In the Christian experience, however, the central revelation of Jesus Christ must eventually enter in. Christology is now a central concern to liberation theology, and Sobrino demonstrates how this is so.

The liberation theologians agree on a radically new method for doing theology. They prefer to begin from the strident cry in their common experience which is filled with pain and oppression. So often it results from the macro-structures. They go to the people themselves and recognize the dehumanization that takes place. Reflecting upon the experience as it is and not what it should be, they raise questions about what salvation in Christ means and implies. Bringing reflection to bear upon action is called praxis. Rather than an approach which is often identified with German idealism that begins from the top down, these theologians prefer to begin from the bottom up and let thought spring from action. Praxis is not to be confused with practice or being practical. Praxis combines practice with theory together in reflection and begins from action. To this end, the basic Christian communities which take the ordinary experience of the people and then ask for their reflection upon it in their terms and hopes offer a fitting example of praxis in the concrete.

By the immersion into praxis, a raising of consciousness usually results. People begin to recognize the injustice of the structures within which they live and work. "Conscientization," which sounds better in Portuguese than in English, describes this process. Usually a recognition of powerlessness, dependence, and frustration in all its ugliness follows. The revolutionary turning upside down of these structures searches for a better life through a utopian vision of what can be. While Marx, Mao, and others offer visions of society, so does Jesus Christ. The Kingdom of God that Jesus preached and lived in his person addressed changes by offering a vision of humanization based on love of God and neighbor that is profoundly practical and easily understandable.

The theologian's task to formulate the Christian experience in living concepts that appropriately address a culturally diverse and unique situation is a challenge. Transposed answers from the European soil are resisted as dead concepts, unable to bring forth the life necessary within divergent people and culture of Latin America to make Christ speak today. A grassroots theology must fundamentally be faithful to itself and its experience of Christ. Liberation theology is by no means an isolationist theology, but like a growing identity in a believer coming to maturity, this theology must finally take responsibility for the Gospel in a particular region. Deeper commitment to faith which does justice is required, and in the process the Kingdom becomes realized as Jesus preached it for all people.

For liberation theologians, the central experience of who Jesus is today is liberator. As Christ was committed to the poor and oppressed, the marginal and outcast, so must the Gospel be if it is to be preached in its fullness. In fact, liberation theologians say that unless one experiences the Gospel as siding with the poor, one does not know the Gospel. Love must not speak eloquent words; it must show itself in deeds. Love brings justice and rightfully belongs to everyone. Faith then does justice. In its Gospel fullness, love also concerns itself with the dehumanizing conditions of people and commits itself to overturning those structures. If there is no commitment to Christ's love, what kind of Gospel is preached? Only one of convenience. The Kingdom of God that Jesus preached, especially proclaimed in the Sermon on the Mount, calls for a humanized social structure of truth, justice, and love.

The Gospel message calls us to be disciples of Christ. Discipleship represents the role of the believer. To be a disciple is to follow Christ. How does one follow Christ in today's world? Only when one identifies with Christ in his love and concern does one begin to understand discipleship. Doing Christ-like actions which spring from the Spirit poured out upon us, as the Acts of the Apostles describes, leads us to Christ today. Liberation theology calls for a discipleship in praxis as the beginning of theological reflection. Participation in the deeds of Christ will certainly remove some of the scales from our blinded eyes and let us see the dehumanizing situation that robs us of our living God's life. Christ is the center of this conversion of life and the suffering Christ is the one whom people of oppressed conditions can identify with. He is a fellow sufferer who brought liberation for God and neighbor. This is not materialism but a profound understanding of the socio-politico-economic demands of Christian love.

Liberation theology in the third world countries finds that economic determinism, colonialism, and the struggle for a better human situation make common cause with Marxist analysis. Christianity and Marxism are two strong contenders for a utopian vision: for Christ, the Kingdom already here in Jesus but not yet completed, and, for Marx, a utopia of the proletariat. The Marxist analysis of economic determiners has provided insight into the laws of society and the situation that the third world finds itself. The question remains open whether the Marxist vision must also be part of the analysis. Liberation theologians do not propose a Marxian utopia but the Christian Kingdom of God instead. An unabashed use of Marx has worried some that these countries are heading toward an atheistic society because they fail to examine the conclusions of Marx. Whether this is true remains an open and serious question. What is not an open question, however, is the impact that economics has on a people. Structures can be evil and yet no one person is responsible for it. Such a generalized world of evil cannot be allowed to exist or encouraged or cooperated with. Structures must work for good on every level. If not, then they must be changed even if it involves revolutionary efforts. Paraphrasing the Gospel message, people do not exist for the sake of the structure but the structure for the sake of people.

One caution needs expression. Revolutionary efforts are not isolated events. One country cannot remain aloof or isolated from the world community. The world community is intertwined, interdependent, and inescapably involved. Liberation theology is not for one country but for all people and places.

How does Sobrino use his theological method? In a situation where so much pain is evident, the suffering of the people makes a strident call from which to begin. This is a different starting point than existentialism. Liberation theology sides with the poor, oppressed, victimized in order to determine which questions are important and how they are to be raised. Analyzing the socio-politico-economic roots of the problem on the one hand, and gathering the faithful together to speak their understanding and commitment to Jesus on the other, these theologians discern the way of living the Kingdom of God. By constant reference to the Scriptures and lived experience, the consciousness of what is and what should be is illuminated. Once consciousness has been raised, appropriate action that should be taken is determined by the community. Discipleship, living in action what is professed in word, is supported and encouraged. The concepts, feelings, and understanding of Jesus Christ emerge now from the people and in their own terms. Theology is not to stamp ready-made expression upon them. Thus Jesus as liberator best expresses who Christ is for these believers.

What do Sobrino and liberation theology contribute to theology today? Liberation theology, which began from Latin America but whose insights have crossed cultural boundaries and is now being universalized under the name "political theology," uses socio-politico-economic analysis for an understanding of religious experience. More than anyone else, the liberation theologians have stressed the role of social scientific appraisal of macro-structures in the study of theology. Hence, since religious experience is set in the cement of cultural structures and values, theology cannot ignore the role these conditions play. Their second contribution is the concept of praxis for doing theology. The third contribution is their attention to the cry of the poor. Only by an insertion of the person into the real conditions of oppression, pain and suffering can theology be credible and the Gospel realized. Evangelization therefore receives a strong boost in their theology. Discipleship remains the characteristic response of the Christian.

Liberation theology remains a young and developing method that has already influenced theology around the world. Latin American theologians are the first to say that they are venturing forth on uncharted waters and that their findings belong first and foremost to Latin America. Other countries and regions need to analyze their own situations and respond accordingly. Therefore, and interesting for us, more than any other theology we have studied, liberation theology really exports not a content but a method. For being so young, it has already had a major influence upon theology.

Conclusion

From the variety of methods presented we can see common traits emerging that give us the character of method's concern today. For the sake of explanation, I have lumped together a particularly clear concern with two theologians. Together the two present differing yet complementary aspects of a given question. I do not want to give the impression that other theologians are not aware nor concerned about a particular problem; often they are. But the emphasis one method gives to a factor (e.g., sociological evidence) makes a great difference in the interpretation of the data. That is why I have kept two theologians and their methods together. My hope is to show that within the same concern, two radical approaches in method may be taken. This is all by way of demonstrating that a method is a tool in the hands of competent theologians by which they search out the truth of a life of faith as they understand it.

There are some important commonalities in the methods we have taken. The first is extremely important and we have traced it through each theologian's work. From the question of the vision that each theologian possesses, we can identify a commitment to life that is not exhausted by material, scientific, or ideological reductionisms. Each theologian holds to what I prefer to call a sacramental view of life and consequently of reality: i.e., that this world is not the entire explanation of reality. There is another dimension which cuts through, permeates, and encompasses this world and we call it not as an object but as a person—God. Each theologian adheres to symbol as important to theology. Each one teases, points to, discloses, cajoles, and investigates this reality. Rahner uses theological anthropology, Lonergan knowing, Macquarrie polarities, Tillich correlation, Tracy interpretation, Meland appreciative awareness, Schillebeeckx mediated immediacy, and Sobrino liberation. The world and the individual as sacrament describes the holiness encountered in reality which is salvific. The reality of God is described by Rahner as Mystery, Lonergan as Being-in-love, Macquarrie as Being-itself, Tillich as Ultimate Concern, Tracy as Holy Other, Meland as Goodness not our own, Schillebeeckx as Grace, and Sobrino as Liberation. Each believes that God interacts with us and we with God through ourselves and world.

The second commonality is more specific than the first in the confidence that the activities of the mind are able to penetrate reality. Whereas animals develop instincts, humans devise methods. A method extends the person to explain and explore the world around him or her. Methods form habits that remind us of things we have forgotten, tell us to look this way and that, and when to look, when we are done, and when to revise what we have found. These theologians of method tell us the importance of the human person (Rahner), conversion (Lonergan), connection to the world (Tillich), importance of tradition (Macquarrie), the manner of responsible interpretation (Tracy), developing internal and external relations (Meland), eradicating suffering (Schillebeeckx), and the socio-politico-economic factors involved in human faith (Sobrino).

The third commonality is the interpretation of data from a particular starting point. With the plurality of methods, the starting point must be made clear for all to see. A method is not forced to begin in one place. Uniformity of starting points is not the value in theology as it once was. Rahner uses Thomism influenced by Kant and Heidegger; Lonergan has written his own philosophical underpinnings; Tillich and Macquarrie rely upon existentialist categories; Tracy devises a hermeneutical schema; Meland roots himself in process-relational categories; Schillebeeckx uses French sociological analysis; and Sobrino uses Marxist analysis of society, politics, and economics.

Today we can recognize that a plurality of methods in fact exists. The difficult question is: How can the variety of starting points and their interpretations be related to one another? Are all methods equally as good? Are all equally revealing of the truth? This is a difficult question that is unresolved and remains a central challenge to theologians of method. Lonergan in his appeal to the mind, Tillich and Macquarrie in the existentialist's insistent need, Tracy and Meland to the universality of human experience, and Schillebeeckx and Sobrino to suffering—each theologian acknowledges the difficulty and offers his contribution toward a common unity. The reality is that theologians are writing more about method precisely to open avenues of dialogue and to seek contributions from whatever discipline. While many starting points can be tolerated, every theologian must come clean on his or her starting point. Realistically, the starting point should be able to be critiqued by the method, call it into question, and improve it. After the starting point is surfaced, method will not allow sloppy reasoning or misapplication of the findings. The principles of coherency and adequacy must apply and can be examined by anyone interested so that theologians actually do what they say they will do.

A fourth commonality is the insistence that Scripture studies be integrated into all theology. Scripture no longer serves as a prooftext but as a document that exists in its own right. Rahner calls for a new area that he calls biblical theology, Lonergan unites Scripture to every step of his method, Tillich brings Scripture to the modern world as an answer, Macquarrie centers his tradition upon it, Tracy correlates Christian texts with human experience and language, Meland stresses its enduring empowerment as a legacy, Schillebeeckx founds the experience of Jesus in it, and Sobrino finds the Scriptures an unleashed liberating power for justice. Perhaps more than any other feature, these theologians' use of Scripture separates them from their predecessors.

A fifth commonality is the irreducible unity between Christianity and humanization. Instead of a secularism which separates the world from God, these theologians find God's self-communication through the world in a sacramental way. Rahner emphasizes hominisation, Lonergan conversion to being in love, Tillich the new being, Macquarrie letting be, Tracy incarnational symbols, Meland the creative passage, Schillebeeckx mediated immediacy, and Sobrino discipleship. In each case, God calls us through his immanent and transcendent relationship with us and our world.

A sixth commonality is the practical nature of theology. Far from being a work done in an ivory tower, theology leads the believer to live better and deeper faith. Rahner calls for the use of authentic freedom, Lonergan finishes his method with communications, Tillich emphasizes the courage to be, Macquarrie invites the believer to let be, Tracy ends his method with practical theology, Schillebeeckx encourages performative theology, and Sobrino relies upon praxis. Whatever contributions theology makes, it finally highlights the summons of God for us to live in unconditional surrender to his salvation.

A seventh and last commonality follows from what has just been said: each theologian searches for God in the modern world and lets God dictate where he will be found. Rahner and Lonergan locate the search in the openness of the human person, Tillich and Macquarrie in the questions arising from the modern world, Tracy and Meland in religious experience, and Schillebeeckx and Sobrino in the structures of society.

One conclusion that we can arrive at is that no one method can exhaust the richness of God's dealings with us. Theologians who work on method offer a valuable contribution to scholars and hence serve the Gospel. Since each method will be partial, it is up to us to evaluate the contributions that each one makes. As a technical and abstract work of specialists, methods will require other specialists to help interpret any implications. The bottom line is that methods belong to all of us and serve our search for understanding faith.

Notes

Chapter 1

1. See Otto Muck, *The Transcendental Method* (N.Y.: Herder and Herder, 1960).

2. Karl Rahner, *Foundations of Christian Faith: An Introduction to the Idea of Christianity* (N.Y.: Seabury Press, 1978).

3. The concept of mystery is essential to Rahner's theology. See *Foundations,* pp. 44–90.

4. See Rahner's philosophical work *Spirit in the World* (N.Y.: Herder and Herder, 1968), and *Foundations,* pp. 3–24.

5. For the Christocentric nature of his theology cf. *Foundations,* pp. 176–322.

6. Rahner, *Hearers of the Word* (N.Y.: Herder and Herder, 1969), and *Foundations,* pp. 24–44.

7. Bernard Lonergan, *Method in Theology* (N.Y.: Herder and Herder, 1972). For Lonergan's evaluation of Muck on transcendental method, cf. p. 13n.4.

8. *Ibid.,* pp. 13–14.

9. Lonergan's thorough treatment is in *Insight: A Study of Human Understanding* (London: Longmans, Green and Co., 1957).

10. Lonergan did not originally specify an affective conversion but added it later.

11. *Method,* pp. 125–145.

Chapter 2

1. John Macquarrie, *Principles of Christian Theology* (N.Y.: Scribner, 2nd edition, 1977).

2. *Ibid.,* pp. 33–39 for a formal discussion of method.

3. For a discussion of liberal and neo-orthodox developments see Sydney Ahlstrom, *Theology in America* (N.Y.: Bobbs-Merrill, 1967) and David Tracy's discussion in *Blessed Rage for Order,* cf. chapter 3 below, n. 4.

4. Paul Tillich, *Systematic Theology* (Chicago: University of Chicago Press, 1951, 1957, 1963, 3 vols.).

5. *Ibid.,* Vol. 1, introduction for his definition of correlation.

6. Tillich also uses the Apostle Paul's description of Christ as the New Adam to designate the same reality.

Chapter 3

1. For a readable account of the American empirical tradition see John E. Smith, *Experience and God* (N.Y.: Oxford University Press, 1968) or his *The Analogy of Experience* (N.Y.: Harper and Row, 1973).

2. David Tracy, *Blessed Rage for Order: The New Pluralism in Theology* (N.Y.: Seabury Press, 1975) and *The Analogical Imagination: Christian Theology and the Culture of Pluralism* (N.Y.: Crossroad, 1981).

3. *Order,* pp. 64–90.

4. *Ibid.,* pp. 22–42 for discussion of the five models.

5. *Imagination,* pp. 1–46 for treatment of the three audiences.

6. Bernard E. Meland, *Faith and Culture* (N.Y.: Oxford University Press, 1953); *The Realities of Faith: The Revolution in Cultural Form* (N.Y.: Oxford University Press, 1962); and *Fallible Forms and Symbols: Discourses on Method for a Theology of Culture* (Philadelphia: Fortress Press, 1976).

7. For an analysis of Meland's appreciative awareness see J. J. Mueller, *Faith and Appreciative Awareness: The Cultural Theology of Bernard E. Meland* (Washington, D.C.: University Press of America, 1981).

8. For the definition of Creative Passage and its importance see *Fallible Forms,* p. xiii.

9. *Ibid.,* p. 173 for the definition of witnesses of faith.

10. For a detailed explanation of these steps see Mueller, pp. 111–122.

Chapter 4

1. Edward Schillebeeckx, *Jesus: An Experiment in Christology* (N.Y.: Seabury Press, 1979); and *Christ: The Experience of Jesus as Lord* (N.Y.: Seabury Press, 1980). A third volume is also projected which will carry on the work of the previous two volumes.

2. *Christ,* pp. 670–731.

3. *Ibid.,* pp. 820–821 for the importance of salvation as performative.

4. *Ibid.,* pp. 744–762.

5. *Ibid.,* p. 809–821 for a discussion of "mediated immediacy." Although not an original phrase by Schillebeeckx, it takes on a vibrant contemporary content through him.

6. While many descriptions of the Latin American situation now exist, the classic presentation for theology was Gustavo Gutierrez, *A Theology of Liberation* (Maryknoll, N.Y.: Orbis, 1973).

7. Jon Sobrino, *Christology at the Crossroads: A Latin American Approach* (Maryknoll, N.Y.: Orbis Books, 1978).

Bibliography

1. Karl Rahner

Rahner, Karl, *Foundations of Christian Faith: An Introduction to the Idea of Christianity.* N.Y.: Seabury Press, 1978.

Rahner, Karl, *Hearers of the Word.* N.Y.: Herder and Herder, 1969.

A Rahner Reader. Edited by Gerald A. McCool. London, Darton, Longman and Todd, 1975.

A World of Grace. Edited by Leo J. O'Donovan. N.Y.: Seabury Press, 1980.

Weger, Karl-Heinz, *Karl Rahner: An Introduction to His Theology.* N.Y.: Seabury Press, 1980.

For an application of Rahner's work, see James J. Bacik, *Apologetics and the Eclipse of Mystery.* Notre Dame: Notre Dame Press, 1980. The first two chapters in John Shea, *The Stories of God: An Unauthorized Biography.* Chicago: Thomas More Press, 1978.

2. Bernard J. F. Lonergan

Lonergan, Bernard, *Method in Theology.* N.Y.: Herder and Herder, 1972.

A Second Collection: Papers. Edited by Wm. F. J. Ryan and Bernard J. Tyrrell. London: Darton, Longman and Todd, 1974.

Crowe, Frederick E., *The Lonergan Enterprise.* Cambridge: Cowley Publications, 1980. (Originally given as the St. Michael's Lectures, Gonzaga University 1979.)

For an application of Lonergan's method, see Frederick E. Crowe, *Theology of the Christian Word,* N.Y.: Paulist Press, 1978.

3. John Macquarrie

Macquarrie, John, *Principles of Christian Theology.* N.Y.: Scribner, 2nd edition, 1977.

Macquarrie, John, *Existentialism.* Philadelphia: Westminster, 1972.

Macquarrie, John, *Thinking About God.* N.Y.: Harper and Row, 1975.

4. Paul Tillich

Tillich, Paul, *Systematic Theology.* Chicago: University of Chicago Press, 1951, 1957, 1963. 3 vols.

McKelway, Alexander, *The Systematic Theology of Paul Tillich.* Richmond: John Knox Press, 1964.

Ambruster, Carl: *The Vision of Paul Tillich.* N.Y.: Sheed and Ward, 1967.

5. David Tracy

Tracy, David, *Blessed Rage for Order: The New Pluralism in Theology.* N.Y.: Seabury Press, 1975.

Tracy, David, *The Analogical Imagination: Christian Theology and the Culture of Pluralism.* N.Y.: Crossroad, 1981.

6. Bernard E. Meland

Meland, Bernard, *Fallible Forms and Symbols: Discourses on Method for a Theology of Culture.* Philadelphia: Fortress Press, 1976.

Mueller, J. J., *Faith and Appreciative Awareness: The Cultural Theology of Bernard E. Meland.* Washington, D.C.: University Press of America, 1981.

Journal of Religion, Oct. 1980, Vol. 60, #4, an entire issue dedicated to the work of Meland.

7. Edward Schillebeeckx

Schillebeeckx, Edward, *Jesus: An Experiment in Christology.* N.Y.: Seabury Press, 1979.

Schillebeeckx, Edward, *Christ: The Experience of Jesus as Lord.* N.Y.: Seabury Press, 1980.

Schillebeeckx, Edward, *Interim Report on the Books Jesus and Christ.* N.Y.: Crossroad, 1981.

8. Jon Sobrino

Sobrino, Jon, *Christology at the Crossroads: A Latin American Approach.* Maryknoll, N.Y.: Orbis Press, 1978.

Boff, Leonardo, *Jesus Christ Liberator.* Maryknoll, N.Y.: Orbis Books, 1978.

Hellwig, Monika, *Jesus, The Compassion of God.* Wilmington, Delaware: Glazier, 1983.

For other theologians of method see (in chronological order):

Harvey, Van A., *The Historian and the Believer.* N.Y.: Macmillan, 1966.

Ogden, Schubert, *The Reality of God.* N.Y.: Harper and Row, 1966.

Gilkey, Langdon, *Naming the Whirlwind: The Renewal of God Language.* N.Y.: Bobbs-Merrill, 1969.

Nygren, Anders, *Meaning and Method.* Philadelphia: Fortress Press, 1972.

Kaufman, Gordon, *An Essay in Theological Method.* Missoula: Scholars Press, 1975.

Other Books in this Series